T·R·I·A·T·H·L·O·N
A·TRIPLE·FITNESS·SPORT

SALLY
EDWARDS

Contemporary Books, Inc.
Chicago

Library of Congress Cataloging in Publication Data

Edwards, Sally, 1947–
    Triathlon : a triple fitness sport.

    Includes index.
    1. Triathlon—Training.   2. Triathlon—Miscellanea.
I. Title.
GV1060.7.E38   1983   796.4   83-1882
ISBN 0-8092-5555-3

Published by Contemporary Books, Inc.
180 North Michigan Avenue, Chicago, Illinois 60601
Manufactured in the United States of America
Library of Congress Catalog Card Number: 83-1882
International Standard Book Number: 0-8092-5555-3

Published simultaneously in Canada by
Beaverbooks, Ltd.
150 Lesmill Road
Don Mills, Ontario M3B 2T5
Canada

contents

Capture the moment
Carry the day
Stay with the chase
As long as you may
Follow the dreamer,
The fool and the sage
Back to the days of
The innocent age.

Source: Dan Fogelberg,
"The Innocent Age."

LEAGUE OF AMERICAN WHEELMEN

1983

NATIONAL CENTURY

This certifies that

_____

has completed an official League of American Wheelmen National

Century Month event by bicycling _____ miles in _____

hours, _____ minutes, on the _____ day of September, 1983.

_____   _____
city   state   club sponsoring event

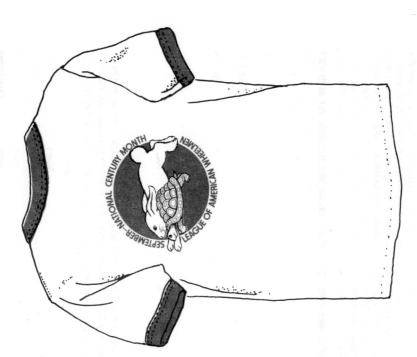

Congratulations!

You have just earned a National Century patch . . . and in recognition of your accomplishment may now proudly wear an exclusive League of American Wheelmen PATCHIRT!

The distinctive PATCHIRT—offered for the first time ever this month—features the same tortoise and hare design that appears on your National Century patch on the back, and has a small tortoise on the front (where some folks wear an alligator). The top quality 50/50 cotton/polyester shirt is white with red trim, colorfully silk screened in red, green and black.

Special member savings

League of American Wheelmen members   **$4.95**

plus $1.00 postage & handling per shirt

Non-members   **$7.00**

plus $1.00 postage & handling per shirt

Non-members can join now!

If you are not a League member, you can join now and save 29% on your PATCHIRT. Fill out the application and get great savings on your PATCHIRT—plus a guarantee of more great cycling as a League of American Wheelmen member!

acknowledgments

The author shares the credit for this book with the following contributors:

Writing Assistance:	Steve Woodcock, John Lehrer
Production:	Jo Sumner
Art:	Michael Welch, Harmon Oscar Nelson III
Critique:	Mo Sproul, Mike Fitzwater, Jerry Hinsdale, Barbara Douglas, Mike Eaton, Charity Kenyon, and many others.
Triathletes:	Elizabeth Jansen, Maryann Truitt, Lori Brusati
Resource:	Greg Peterson, Bill Thomas, Cheri Wolpert
Supporters:	Gaye Edwards, Jerrylee Vanderhurst, Sharron Brockman

I am grateful to my many athlete friends who coached, trained, and shared their enthusiasm with me. They travel these pages in heart, mind, and muscle.

preface

Serious athletes have a continual flow of questions about staying fit, improving athletic performance, and winning races. They seem to have an almost insatiable appetite for the secrets of success in sports.

There is a popular notion that sports heroes know certain truths about technique and motivation. Some ambitious contenders think that if these heroes would but divulge these eternal, hidden, unspoken formulas for success that they, too, could cross the finish line first and win gold and glory.

The idea that there is some magic combination of strategies and tactics, that sports achievement is more than talent, luck, and dedication, has resulted in the spouting of many diverse philosophies, each with a founder eager to sell his secrets.

What these gurus and their students refuse to admit is that there are no secrets. There is no magic element that they can buy at a shoe store, eat at a health food restaurant, inherit from genes, or chant hypnotically. There are, however, a few sound, common-sense principles champions follow.

These principles are the subject of this book.

1

hawaii, 1981: making it look easy

Imagine yourself a slim, 33-year-old woman standing in the Kailua-Kona beach among heavily muscled women and men who tower above you, each clad only in a swatch of spandex nylon. The dim light of early morning barely illuminates a boat with orange sails more than a mile offshore. You are about to swim to that boat and back, attempting the first leg of Hawaii's 1981 Ironman Triathlon World Championship. A TV crew is taking in the scene; the announcer gives final instructions. Your muscles quiver as you anticipate the day ahead. The race is about to begin.

I was that person. As co-owner of Fleet Feet Sports, Inc., fitness is my business. As a woman, athletic activity is part of my liberation. My personal and professional interests are entwined in a lifestyle that makes the running trail my office and my office a place to savor life. Looking back on my triathlon ordeal, I have chosen to tell my story in the third person, as though I were another person. I was, in a sense, transformed by the event, as is anyone who chooses to experience the outer limits of her abilities and endurance. This book is about making that choice.

#   #   #

For three years Sally had anticipated that morning in Hawaii. The

Moments of anticipation before the start of the IRONMAN, triathletes are preparing both mentally and physically for the long day ahead.

path to that sandy beach began with a simple interest in sports, which eventually developed into a passion—an obsession, some would say. Graduate study at Berkeley in physical education gave her an academic foundation in fitness, with a master's thesis appropriately written on the causes of muscle fatigue. Then she read Ken Cooper's work on aerobics, written in the late 1960s, and she was off and running. Eventually Sally entered a road race. She did well and discovered that she liked the competition; she liked to win.

The races became longer and more frequent. First seven miles, then 10+, 20+, and the 26.2-mile marathon. Next a 50-miler, then 75, and then the Western States 100-Mile Endurance Run. Next she, another sportswoman, and a horse ran the Levi's Ride & Tie, and soon after that she entered her first triathlon. Sally met both success and failure in these contests, enticed ever onward by her need to progress, to meet each new challenge, to build with each effort a foundation for confronting the next one. She acquired a unique kind of self-understanding that comes from triumph and disappointment.

That morning, standing on the Pacific beach, Sally found herself reciting some of the hard-earned principles ingrained from the experience of those previous competitions: Don't feel intimidated by the starting field; don't wander into the deadly riptide of reasons to fail—"Why didn't I prepare more," "The competition looks in better shape," and "I should have lost more body fat." She quelled her doubt and changed her focus, admiring the physiques of the men and women who were confident that they could power themselves through the choppy ocean for 2.4 miles, then pedal for 112 miles in muggy heat, and then run 26.2 miles to the third and final finish line.

Never before had she tried to do what she would attempt today. Her preparation for the swim had consisted of nothing more than laps in the YMCA pool. Yet here was the ocean—deep, salty, rough, without lanes, and full of creatures. A predictable nervousness caused her to shiver despite the tropical warmth. Can one prepare fully for the unfamiliar? Was her anxiety shared by her tanned and muscled competitors?

The start was minutes away. Some of the men strode confidently into the ocean and swam to the starting line, where they treaded water while awaiting a signal blast from the starting cannon. A power boat full of film crews and celebrities took position as the countdown continued. The sun had just risen.

Sally knew that anything could go wrong in the 141 miles ahead. Any number of oversights, little errors, and fateful intrusions might crop up along the way. The tropical sun was a potential problem, shining all day on a skin paled by Sacramento's fog. For the swim she had applied zinc oxide to the back of her knees, the most exposed part of her body during the first event. Then the first mistake occurred—the slick residue on her fingers caused the strap on her swim goggles to slip through its buckles. Frantically, with only seconds until the start, she sought help from the head of the

Arms churning, legs fluttering, the triathlon begins.

swim race, who loaned her another set of goggles. This time she carefully avoided smearing them with the grease on her hands.

The cannon boomed; the race was on. Quickly, she hugged her closest friend, business partner, and sister triathlete, Elizabeth Jansen, and they walked into the water together. The hard chargers were already in motion, arms flying, water splashing. They looked like a school of sardines, its wake widening as more entered the ocean, 350 in all.

Sally tried to keep up with Elizabeth, but her friend was the more powerful swimmer and a tenacious competitor. Elizabeth pulled away. There was no shortage of other bodies in the crowded water, with the fast ones swimming over the backs of the slow, the slow ones flutter-kicking in the faces of the fast. Sally's borrowed goggles did not fit well, and she had to stop frequently and tread water as she adjusted them, each time smearing the lenses with more grease. Her target, the boat with two orange sails, became but a colorful blur.

A succession of outrigger canoes spaced 500 yards apart defined the path of the swim. Aboard the canoes were volunteer lifeguards with surfboards, ready to haul in swimmers in trouble. A large, white fishing boat marked the halfway point. She would pass it twice—once on the way out and once on the way back to shore. At the end of the string of canoes loomed the large glass-bottomed tourist boat with orange sails.

Sally felt relieved when she reached the turnaround. The boat was crammed with spectators and photographers yelling encouragement to the swimmers, who could hear only garble and splash. Next to her, a swimmer did not complete the turn around the boat and headed out toward the open sea. Another reminder of a hard-learned lesson, she thought: Do not follow those in front; follow your own inclinations. She circled the boat and began to swim— the canoes were again to her right—holding close to the line defining the shortest distance between the two most important points at the moment—her body and the shore.

Past the halfway mark, the weight of doubt sloughed off into the salty water. She was certain she could finish the swim; now maybe she could pick up the pace. Breathing harder, feeling pain high across her shoulders, concentrating on her form, she began to stroke faster and moved up through the field. Then, in the distance, she saw through her smeared goggles a few contestants walking up the boat ramp onshore. The finish was imminent.

Time for a here-and-now check of all systems. Sally asked her body how it was doing, and the different systems answered one at a time. Feet and legs? Not working hard yet. Arms? Tired, but sturdy enough to hold on to handlebars. Eyes? Unaffected by salt water—the goggles were working. Kinesthetics? All motions smoothly in cadence, muscles working with—not against—each other. Endurance? Pace strong, fires burning steadily, no sign of fatigue. Just keep moving in good form and you'll get there.

Sally had completed the initial leg of the Hawaii "gruelathon." Quite a contrast to her first triathlon in Lodi, California, three years earlier. Then the events had been much shorter and in a different

Pat Hines was the fastest woman swimmer at the IRONMAN, February 1982.

sequence. The footrace had been first, a mere three miles, followed by a seven-mile bicycle race and then a swim through a swampy frog pond that the Lodi locals called a lake. She had led the run and had been the first woman off her bicycle. But though she had begun the two-thirds-of-a-mile swim with a five-minute lead, she had ended up the fifth female finisher. Each sweep of her stroke had reaped a harvest of pond lilies. Sally didn't like swimming through a swamp, but she liked finishing fifth even less.

Remembering the Lodi triathlon, she prepared to stagger up the boat ramp as her sense of balance readjusted to land. Her inner ear responded and stabilized those wobbly legs. As Sally pulled herself out of the water and regained her dry-land footing, she broke into a trot. In fresh-water showers, she joined the muscled bodies she had so admired earlier.

The shower was quick. No time for idle relexation! The race was still on; the clock would not stop until she had finished all three events. Briskly but carefully, Sally washed the sand and salt out of her hair. If any salt remained, she might sweat it into her eyes later. As she left the shower, a volunteer passed her the blue bag printed with the large number 104, the same number scrawled in felt pen on her shoulders for identification during the swim. Everything read 104 that day, it seemed, even the temperature.

Dressing quickly, Sally downed a cup of water and grabbed two bananas before sighting bicycle 104 racked in space 104. Hers was easy to find, since most of the 350 racks were empty. The machine, a French LeJeune, was a beauty. She had borrowed it from a friend in lieu of purchasing her own for $1,000 or more. The frame was 25 inches, for its 6'3" owner—she didn't know about the disadvantages of having the wrong bike size. She did know that it was light and fast.

The crowd had kept up its enthusiasm. The first cyclists had raced away 40 minutes earlier, but their claps and yells resounded strongly in her heart and made her feel like a winner as she set off. Sally looked at her watch. It read one hour, 27 minutes.

The second race was under way; she knew that, with luck, it would be well into the hot afternoon before she would dismount.

There were seven women in front of her—Shawn Wilson, a fellow Sacramentan, was in the lead. This was to be expected, since Shawn was a swimmer. But her strongest event was over.

At first the morning was cool, a beautiful time for a leisurely bike ride through town. This course, though, stretched far out from Kona along a black asphalt highway laid atop a bleak, black lava flow. The blackness of road and stone gradually absorbed the sun's heat, and soon the landscape shimmered. Sally felt like a little pat of butter in an immense black cast-iron frying pan. She was not fully confident on a bike, had never participated in a bicycle race, and knew little about repairs or maintenance, technique or training. Yet she was able to shake her doubts. Here-and-now is all that matters, she told herself. No gain from wallowing in excuses to fail.

No pit crews were allowed, since self-reliance was an essential part of the triathlon mystique. Contestants had to be responsible for their own food (if they wanted something different from what the officials provided), equipment, and repairs. Sally had tucked two extra sew-up tires under the bicycle saddle and had learned how to change a flat only the week before. Fortunately, her new knowledge never had to be tested. Her friend, Elizabeth, with tougher high-pressure clinchers, had all the tire problems—two flats at mile 65 on the black asphalt highway in the black lava desert in 100-degree-plus heat. It was a stroke of bad luck, but the determined Elizabeth had by no means finished playing out her hand.

It was noon when Sally reached the turnaround point in the small town of Hawi. Spectators and aid station volunteers cared for the contestants. All competitors had to stop for a mandatory weight check. Sally dismounted her red LeJeune and ate yet another banana. Someone announced that she had gained two pounds. She knew the scales were not accurate, as the effects of lost body fluids should have been a weight loss, not a gain. Race officials had provided bananas, oranges, and donuts. Sally knew better than to pick oranges or donuts—oranges are too high in acid for easy digestion, and deep-fried donuts are high in fat, a poor food source

At the early morning stages of the long bicycle ride, your shadow is equally as long—such is the distance of the day.

for high performance. Sally would have preferred her special diet of baby food or a sandwich. So, for hours she ate only bananas, all day and into the night—boring, bland bananas.

Sally passed four women riders during the arduous trip. Her spirits were high as she rode through the afternoon, surrounded by landscapes of black lava fields radiating waves of heat. Constantly exposing herself to the sun took its toll: Sally became dehydrated. As John Howard, the first-place man, was beginning the marathon race along the same road, Sally was 14 miles from the finish of the bike race and still pedaling. He was wearing a bicycle cap and was shining, shirtless in the sunlight, from the water he poured over his body.

Sally's only thought near the end of the bike leg was to get it over with. Her rear felt as if the bicycle seat would need to be surgically removed, and her shoulders ached from the unaccustomed tension of keeping her head up for seven hours. Her quadriceps—primary bicycle muscles—sputtered spastically. She was just plain tired. The pain subsided when she concentrated on it, a technique learned from Shiatsu therapy for years of sciatic nerve problems in her hips. Only one steep but short hill was left before she entered the parking lot of the Kona Surf Resort Hotel, one long grind in the lowest gear to the crest, then a coast down the hill. One hundred and twelve miles finished in six hours and 58 minutes.

For Sally the bicycle race—the longest segment of the Hawaii Triathlon in both time and distance—was over. The first male finisher, John Howard, had been a Pan American gold medal winner in cycling. He completed the course in five hours and three minutes. The fastest woman, finishing in six hours and 35 minutes, was Shawn Wilson. Shawn's speed was holding out.

At the finish of the bike ride there were no flags or lines to cross. The 112-mile bike race simply petered out in the hotel parking lot near the tennis courts. Sally's mother and friends were there applauding. After spending seven hours in a fixed position, her muscles always pulling the same way, her bottom glued to the seat, Sally dismounted. As she waddled to the scales to be weighed again, she knew her bicycle seat would be a companion for life. No point in eating any more digusting bananas—she was plugged up at the other end for good.

Race rules state that a contestant must be within 10 percent of starting weight at each weigh station. Sally started at 124 pounds and finished at 120 pounds—a tough way to stay trim. Someone handed her plastic bag number 104—this one held her running clothes. A woman volunteer accompanied her to the dressing room. She told the volunteer she was rather in a rush, lacked modesty, and would appreciate help in stripping and dressing. The volunteer even laced up her Nike racing shoes, as Sally stuffed down another unacceptable banana.

She strode out of the parking lot to start the 26.2-mile run at three o'clock. She knew there were three women in front of her—but running was her forte. Within a mile she passed the third-place woman and advanced with determination to second place. To her surprise, that second-place person was Shawn Wilson, and she was

Sally Edwards leaves the Kona Surf at the start of the running leg, in hot pursuit of the three ironwomen in front of her.

walking. Shawn had never run a marathon before. Sally walked and chatted with her—the encounter was a good excuse to rest at a walking pace. Sally was already deep into her reserve tank, her glycogen low.

After a few minutes Sally broke into a slow run, leaving Shawn behind. The landscape rolled by, almost unseen. Moving more slowly than she had on her bicycle, she noticed the heat more. It seemed to rise from the hot pavement, through her feet and into her upper body. The slight ocean breeze helped, but not much. Her legs were shot—they had no more strength. The bicycle race was taking its toll. The hours of fast, constant pedaling and running had drained her energy. Her will said to run; her legs said to walk.

Near mile six she began to have a sharp abdominal pain that jarred with every step. It was a dry-heave kind of pain. Her stomach was on the verge of rebellion. Probably bananas and bicycle seats. She compromised by alternating mile runs with one-minute walks. The compromise worked; her stomach improved. She passed the halfway point of the run at about 5:00 P.M. Thirteen miles still lay ahead, and there was still a woman in front of her. Linda Sweeney, from Tucson, Arizona, was a 22-year-old marathoner with a PR (personal record) two minutes faster than Sally's own best mark of 2:53. Linda had been 30 minutes ahead at the end of the swim, and halfway through the marathon Linda was still 30 minutes in front.

As the sun started to set, Sally reached the last weigh-in station. Her weight was stable now at 121 pounds. The changes in the light—from hot afternoon brightness, to the reddening sky, to the inevitable darkness—seemed to be a metaphor for Sally's waning energy. She learned that the woman ahead had not faltered in her pace, and there was nothing left that Sally could do to run faster.

Her spirits deteriorated as she became more fatigued. The marathon, her specialty, was now her worst event, because it was last. Darkness added to her gloom, making her feel alone and isolated. It was nighttime now; and with two miles left to the finish, her mind was asking the same question a thousand times over: "Why are you doing this to yourself? You can stop, you know." At that point she knew she would have to reach deep down inside to grab whatever remaining energy and courage she needed to endure. It is a long reach, and it comes close to touching the soul. In this moment of crisis some people crack—others find that no matter how hard the struggle, they can continue to the end. At the 25-mile marker, Sally knew that she could finish the race. The last mile would be her personal victory lap. She would finish her first ultradistance triathlon, the ultimate test of all-around fitness. No matter what her place on the list of finishers, she was first in her self-esteem.

She remembered the scene at the pier when the race had begun early that morning. Now it was dark, the thick dark of a Hawaiian night. She was wearing an orange reflective bib so that she would be visible to passing motorists on that long, lonely black highway. Suddenly, she came upon a crowd of cheering spectators lining the street near the pier where the marathon finished. "Second woman," they were yelling. She remembered one of the rules in her bag of tricks. No matter how tired or how sore you are, regardless of the terrible shape of your feet and bottom, you try to make it look easy. The spectators not only are there to encourage you, but they are also curious to see the faces of the dying. As an experienced gladiator in the arena of endurance sports, she knew that she must make the ordeal look effortless, as if she had just begun. A smile spread across her face—she was elated to be finishing. Her spine straightened; her pace quickened; her feet skipped over the pavement. The crowd was applauding. Light showered down from a tower as the TV crew captured the glory of her triumph. The finish clock stopped—a moment to last a lifetime. A picture in her mind clicked at 12:33:15. She crossed the finish line at 7:30 P.M. with a marathon split time of four hours and 10 minutes.

Two women placed a flower lei around Sally's neck, kissed her in congratulation, and led her to a grassy area where she could sit. She had wondered during each leg of the race how it would feel finally to stop and sit. And now she knew what only another 141-mile triathlon finisher could know. The last event was now over, and she could rest. Masseuses were working on several prone triathletes, and she waited her turn. When the volunteer masseuse asked where the pain was, she could have read off the index to *Gray's Anatomy*.

Her next concern was Elizabeth. The race was not over until it was over for both of them. Though Elizabeth had lost much time on her luckless bicycle ride, she had vowed to continue on through the marathon. She hiked those 26.2 miles in seven hours and 52 minutes and finished 18 hours and 43 minutes after the triathlon had begun. The crowd was gone; the film crew was home in bed;

the masseuses had left long before; the flower leis had all been distributed. But the clock and the finish banner and Sally were still there. Elizabeth, too, remembered the trick—she stood up straight, her feet started running, a smile spread across her face. She made it look really easy, but Sally knew better.

2
triathletics: history and prospects

Generally speaking, a triathlon is any race combining three sports in uninterrupted sequence. Cross-country skiing, kayaking, and roller-skating, for example, could be linked to create a triathlon. For our purposes, however, we will define the triathlon exclusively as a combination of three specific aerobic fitness sports: swimming, bicycling, and running, performed most frequently in that order.

The sequence of events is important for safety reasons. It is safest to swim a long distance when you are fresh (a tired swimmer can drown); it is safest to cycle long distances before you become really fatigued (an exhausted cyclist can collide with other cyclists, cars, pedestrians, or stationary objects); and it is safest to run last (a completely drained runner can always walk).

This arrangement of events is probably not the best for maximizing performance. An upper-body event followed by two lower-body events makes tremendous demands on the legs. A combination with the swim in the middle would allow the legs to rest before being exercised again. But safety precludes this sequence, at least for ultradistance.

A BRIEF HISTORY

The triathlon has little history; it is a newborn babe. The sport started in the 1970s—there are no founders to speak of, no Abner Doubledays of triathlons. Races just cropped up in various communities, many as extensions of bicycle-run or bicycle-swim biathlons held by biking clubs. In Sacramento, California, an event called "The Great Race," which combined biking, kayaking, and running—first initiated as a fundraiser by a local restaurateur—now boasts more than 2,000 biking, kayaking, and running participants.

The Hawaii International Triathlon has taken a new name—The Ironman Triathlon World Championship. This race is now considered the granddaddy of the triathlons. With the longest distance and the hottest climate, the Ironman contest is billed as the premier individual endurance event of the world—a 2.4-mile swim, a 112-mile bike ride, a 26.2-mile run. The distances evolved from three separate races held in Hawaii: the Waikiki Rough-Water Swim, the Around-the-Island Oahu Bicycle Race, and the Honolulu Marathon. In 1981 the race was moved from Oahu to Kona, Hawaii.

In the first race 15 men participated and 12 finished. *Sports Illustrated* featured the race in a 1979 article, and *"ABC's Wide World of Sports"* covered the event in 1980. By 1981 there were 300 men and 22 women participating. The event will continue to grow; the media will pay it more and more attention. In addition, other triathlons will receive television coverage.

The sport is burgeoning to the extent of taking on international proportions. Last year triathlon races were held in Australia and Holland. California seems to be the seedbed, having hosted more triathlons than any other state.

Popularity has its hazards. A certain kind of elitism permeates the sporting community, and there is danger that it will affect triathletics. Many athletes in each specialty feel that their sport requires the most strength, the most endurance, the most speed, the most discrimination in equipment. They are elitists, because they think that outstanding performance or sophisticated equipment makes them superior human beings.

Scott Tinley, February 1982 Ironman Winner. For Scott Tinley, the work paid off—a trophy.

For example, some elitist runners feel that their sport is the most demanding. They strut before the starting line; take cash money under the table so they can maintain their so-called amateur status; ask for handouts, freebies, trips, and equipment; and proclaim running as the second coming on waffle soles.

Swimmers, by contrast, seem to count fewer elitist egos among their number, which is surprising considering how hard good swimmers must work. Top swimmers spend four to six hours in the pool every day, on the average, with double and triple individual workouts. Maybe the confinement of their linear jail— the loneliness of minds cut off from communication with others during those tedious workouts—makes swimmers the true soloists in athletics. They are entitled to feel proud; but in my experience most are quite humble.

Elitist cyclists, though, are the spoiled *creme de la creme* of the lot. Of course, elitist cyclists are in the minority; but just for the experience, you should seek them out to ride with sometime. It's true that their workouts extend for hundreds of miles, and they face danger of the highest degree—death on the roads. Sure, they are working anaerobically much of the time, but they have one ingredient that runners and swimmers do not have—a piece of machinery, the bicycle. They not only compete in physical ability, but also in equipment: frames, accessories, clothes, and the money spent on all of them. Elitist cyclists are crass materialists. They argue for hours over who is the best frame builder, what type of tubing is tops, what combination of accessories is the most efficient, and how to fit a bicycle. They argue over names like Suntour, Campagnolo (Campy), Dura-Ace, Gran-Compe, Wienmann, and Zeus—and they're just talking about brakes! Erudition in trivia.

To be among elitist cyclists, you must have a whole new lexicon of definitions, nicknames, and jargon. They dress beautifully, with special seamless riding shorts that have chamois crotches, special cycling shirts for cutting wind resistance, and other paraphernalia. Cycling is really two sports—touring and racing—each with distinctive needs.

Enter the triathlete. The triathlon requires the best combination

Kim Bushong, considered the Rod Stewart of triathlons, preserves his lead in the February 1982 IRONMAN.

of all three specialties, a balance of sports. Triathletes must be specialists in swimming, biking, and running. They cannot train too much in one sport to the detriment of the others. They are the premier athletes, the only ones entitled to claim all-around fitness, but they are not entitled to the arrogance of elitism.

Who has the right to be a snob in the sports world? Nobody. The person who practices triathletics, however, is certainly entitled to be proud.

Aerobic (cardiovascular) fitness can be developed by training at a level of strenuous exertion in any endurance sport. You can be aerobically fit if you run, swim, or cycle, but single-sport fitness is not enough for full-body muscle vigor. Triathletics require the development of total-body kinesiology—motor skills, muscular strength, and aerobic endurance.

Also, triathletic preparation has added a new dimension to endurance sports—transition training. Workouts must incorporate not only the principles of multisport events but also the way in which the events interrelate. The transition required to hop off a bike and stride off in a pair of running shoes is almost a sport in itself. Muscles must become familiar with drastic shifts in stress and motor patterns. *Linkage* means combining separate elements into a chain. Triathletics is a linkage of three activities into one continuum of whole-body utilization.

Triathletes are the premier aerobic fitness stars, yet they have been labeled wierdos, crazies, and eccentrics who can't resist the lure of a bizarre, excruciating stunt. A recent newspaper item placed triathletes in the lunatic fringe, calling them a bunch of adventurers looking for a thrilling challenge. As you may remember not long ago, sportswriters were saying the same of marathoners.

The triathlete is a new breed in a sport just now reaching adolescence. The number of participants in triathlons is growing, and performances are improving. Triathletes are developing a love for and loyalty to their sport, and the serious ones no longer consider themselves specialists in search of adventure. Rather they are beginning to define themselves as triathletes—disciplined competitors in significant athletic contests. They no longer ask which single sport provides the best conditioning, because they know that each of the three events must be trained for on its own terms and that they must combine training techniques, "crosstrain," if they wish to succeed in triathlons. They are not driven to prove that cyclists or swimmers or runners are the best, for they realize that the sport is more than the sum of its three components. The triathlete, not the specialist, wins the race.

THE APPEAL OF THE TRIATHLON

Why do single-sport athletes switch to the triathlon? The answer is complex. The most frequently offered reason is for the challenge. The specialist leaves a comfortable womb and is born into a whole world of new people, new ideas, new training programs, new experiences. The challenge of learning additional skills, improving performance, balancing development, enduring stress, and

Scott Tinley's physique is a fine product of triple fitness.

competing with the best from other sports disciplines is very seductive. The triathlon is the new frontier of sports, and athletes who have the spirit of explorers and pioneers are challenged by its wide-open prospects.

The 20th-century athlete is hungry—even famished—for adventure. Many sports enthusiasts have sampled skiing, backpacking, tennis, scuba diving, and other activities in their quest for physical and psychological self-mastery. In their youth they were regimented on the school yards and in physical education classes. Soccer, baseball, basketball, football, track and field—none supplied the answers to their athletic needs. After exploring a variety of sports from childhood or adolescence to adulthood, many athletes discover that true adventure is a part of themselves, not the sports they play. That is what triathlons promise: an adventure for the body, an exploration into vast uncharted territory of the self.

To some, the triathlon epitomizes hard-core reality. For many athletes today there is boredom in their workouts—a lack of pizzazz. The triathlon provides these souls with a new sport—one that will take them years to comprehend and master.

Then there are those who want to know the limits of human performance. How much can we do, and how far can we go? What ultimately stops the human being from being able to continue to move, to perform at a level of adequacy? Has the event been designed that challenges our untapped potential? When will the ultimate test of human aerobic talent be created? Even Hawaii's ultradistance triathlon only piques our interest in these still unexplored dimensions.

Inveterate athletes seek out the triathlon because they are in pursuit of total fitness. The triathlon provides avenues for strength, speed, endurance, agility, balance, and kinesthetic skill—the six basic components of physical fitness.

It is an agonizing self-test, an endless moment of truth when the ego must grope for substantiation. Many people will never enter such contests, not because of the effort but because of the risk of self-discovery. The race poses the most frightening question of all: Who am I? Am I an impostor, a self-made failure, a coward, a fool?

Or, can I use the triathlon to bring out my best human qualities? Can I make it a kind of heroic quest? These are the questions that confront you as you stand on the sandy beach in Hawaii, nearly naked and soon to be stripped to the soul.

Of course, not everyone looks at a triathlon this way. To others, it is a game. You take all of your conditioning and all of your adult toys and you play triathlon. The sport is one of fun and lightness, long bicycle rides and picnics with friends, weekends of races and comaraderie. It is a chance to don the suit and show off the body. The spirit of play attracts many athletes to the sport. To take joy in your movement and to discover your potential is a wonderful liberation. Americans these days take their fun very seriously and work hard at leisure. Triathlons are in tune with the times.

We were triathletes as children—most of us had to ride our bikes to school; our parents took us to the pool in the summertime; we ran all day on the playgrounds with the games of tag, gotcha, and one-two-three red light. The child was a balanced athlete, and now the adult wants to return to that early joy, that youthful exuberance, with a mature understanding of the human body.

THE FUTURE OF TRIATHLONS

Americans have a love for sports and a lust for leanness. We are exercise-crazy: More than 105 million of us swim, 69 million of us bicycle, and 35 million of us run. And, of course, we all are addicted to newness.

The groundswell of participants in the sport of triathlons will come from each of the individual sports plus the new inductees who are currently unable to find any fitness program as suitable. The chart that follows offers a clear indication of why this new fitness sport will be growing to astronomical proportions: its source of possible participants comes from three of the four most popular participant sports in America. When you combine the 105 million swimmers with 69.8 million cyclists with 35.7 million runners/joggers, you have a field of 210.5 million participants. There never before has been a new sport with a population base such as this to support its growth and development. We are on the ground level of a triathlon-fitness boom whose time has come: triathlon fever.

These factors assure a healthy future for triathletics. I will venture a few provocative predictions:

- The triathlon will become the second most popular participatory sporting event after 10-k races and marathons. Every major city will host at least one per year.

- The triathlon will become an Olympic sport, possibly replacing the antiquated modern pentathalon (fencing, horseback riding, shooting, running, swimming).

- The triathlon will become a mass media event, with winners becoming celebrities and household names.

- The triathlon will lure many champions from running, swimming, and cycling and thus become the superbowl of endurance sport competition.

- The triathlon will be viewed by the public as the true, all-around fitness contest and will generate superstars more revered and popular than champions in single sports.

- The triathlon will take on international importance with circuits and prize money. Triathletes will earn incomes in six digits for their performances.

- The triathlon will prompt academia to research new methods of training and thus revolutionize the current body of sports knowledge.

- The triathlon will become a major spectator sport in three distinct categories: sprint, middle-distance, and ultradistance. Special stadiums and arena setups combining Olympic-size swimming pools, velodromes, and running tracks will be used for triathlon sprints, which may repeat the sequence of the three events several times.

- A major slick monthly magazine on triathletics will be published and on newsstands throughout the United States, and it will outsell the other three major specialty sport magazines combined.

- Triathletes will be sought for the corporate speaking circuit to promote whole-body aerobics by means of swim-bike-run crosstraining programs.

- Triathlon clubs will be organized to sponsor events, individuals, and ways of meeting other triathletes, similar to the bike, running, and swimming clubs that are their forebears.

- Triathletes will be sought for both product-endorsement contracts and as models for fitness and sports magazines. The triathlete's physique will be considered the new standard for fitness.

The future is happening now. Valerie Silk, race director for the Ironman Triathlon, is discussing the planning of an international circuit of races. A publication, *Swim-Bike-Run,* was first circulated in June 1982, by the publishers of *Swim Swim* magazine. Competitors who develop themselves into all-around aerobic power-houses of speed, strength, and endurance will blaze new trails for the exercise physiologists to follow and chart. Triathletes might improve on their individual endurance sports performances as a result of all-around training. They might develop new ways of refining techniques for the most efficient propulsion. If such developments occur, we will see a far-reaching revolution in training programs with the systematic inclusion of complementary sports into conditioning schedules.

Speed ice skaters, in the off-season, train on bicycles. Beth and Eric Heiden are champions in both. Perhaps someday a triathlete will hold world records in more than one of the three activities— swimming, bicycling, and running.

The fortunes of triathletes will change. Many triathletes are now living at subsistence levels on savings or patronage. Dave Scott,

A triathlete swims-bikes-runs on the edge of his or her maximum physical performance abilities. This is one of the "whys" of triathlon participation: to measure that maximum.

1980 and 1982 Hawaii winner, quit his job to train full-time for the 1982 race. Individuals who sacrificed their livelihood for excellence in triathletics might awaken to new riches. If they win, they may be as sought after as Mark Spitz and Bruce Jenner once were: Movie contracts, commercials, and product endorsements may come their way. This is already happening to John Howard, Scott Tinley, and Kathleen McCartney. As Bruce Jenner is to the anaerobic decathlon, the new triathlon champions will be to the aerobic endurance sports.

I hope that triumphant triathletes in the future will appreciate the race as well as the glory that comes to them. They must have allegiance to the discipline; they must pay homage to their sport. For the sake of triathlons, they cannot afford to bicker and quibble about the superiority of one specialty over another. They must

For Julie Moss at the February 1982 IRONMAN, the finish was so close, yet so far away.

unanimously praise the triathlon as the legitimate test of all-around aerobic fitness.

In this chapter I've indicated a number of reasons why people are becoming attracted to triathlons; but, for me and for other triathlete friends, the reason we love triathlons is a much deeper matter. We like the fitness, the challenge, the new frontiers, the return to our childhood, and the fun. Participation in both the sport and the triathlon lifestyle is a way for us to stay in touch with ourselves. Triathlon fitness, like love, is a way to find our way back to ourselves. The training portion of the lifestyle is who we are *actualized, made real;* the racing portion is like the whipped cream on the cake that you can have and eat, too. It's that time when we reach down deep for what we essentially are.

When Julie Moss collapsed at the finish line of the February 1982

Ironman Triathlon World Championship in Hawaii, she was regarded in two general ways: On the one hand are those who think that in sports we should never be allowed to continue that far into the depths of exhaustion and fatigue and possibly into one of those never-never lands where we could incur permanent physical damage. On the other hand are those of us who believe that if you have the opportunity in life to live through the "ultimate experience," you should do so. There are very few times when you can put yourself on the line, when it's an absolutely clear-cut choice. It's yes or no, succeed or fail, win or lose. If you can prevail and win in a test of both inner strength and physical strength, as Julie did, you possess a power that no one can take away from you. Julie Moss had that chance and made that choice. She said, in effect, "Yes, I will do everything I can to win, and should I fail in that, I *will* cross that finish line to do what I set out to do."

For Julie, the glory was in finishing what she set out to do, even if she were reduced to her hands and knees. When the film cameras are rolling and you know that you are going to be seen around the world in a heroic effort to be first, to be the best, then that once-in-a-lifetime experience is worth all the effort you can direct toward that goal—a permanent memory of reaching into yourself to touch a place you have never touched before and probably never will again. It is that touching that is worth the effort.

When I finally arrived at the finish line at Hawaii and the spotlight blazed gloriously, I heard a voice inside me cheering even louder than the crowd, louder even than the whirl of the helicopters overhead. That voice came from within and clearly announced, "You did it!" That, truly, was the object of my quest—that 141 miles and 12½ hours later I had come into contact with that part of myself that usually lies hidden, elusive, mysterious.

The memory of that feeling is my trophy.

triathlon language

Words come from experiences and reflections on those experiences. Triathlons combine events from already existing sports; but since the whole *is* often greater than the sum of its parts, triathlons produce new athletic experiences. Therefore, we need new words to describe what goes on in a triathlon.

Everybody involved in the sport more or less needs to speak the same language—be they triathletes themselves, sportswriters, sports fans, researchers, or physiologists. They need to have concise, clear terminology at their fingertips. Right now, *Webster's Dictionary* doesn't even list the term *triathlon,* which shouldn't be a surprise, since the sport is so new.

The terms that follow have grown out of the rather brief life span of the sport. Additions will continue to be made as we discover information and experiences. Much of this will come from the tests done by exercise physiologists, who will be measuring performances, analyzing injuries, and trying to describe both. Sports psychologists will be tossing new terms at us to describe the "triathlete bonk," "crosspeaking," and other such phenomena in an attempt to combine specific experiences that relate only to the sport of triathlons.

For now, we can settle on a few commonly accepted terms.

ANAEROBIC THRESHOLD (AT): A condition experienced when exercise intensity reaches a level at which the rate of lactic acid diffusion into the bloodstream exceeds its rate of removal from the blood. In this condition, the body has reached the anaerobic threshold (AT). The AT is usually expressed as the percentage of your maximum oxygen consumption. Well-trained endurance athletes appear to reach their AT when they are working at the 85% to 90% level of maximum oxygen consumption. In the untrained individual, it is common to see AT at between 70% and 75% of maximum oxygen consumption.

BIKE-TO-RUN SYNDROME: This is an inability to run efficiently after the cycle leg of a triathlon probably due to either the shortening of the quadricep muscles from the bike exertion or severe fatigue in those same muscles.

CHANGING CORRALS: The term used by triathlon race directors to describe a room for athletes to change clothes for their next stage.

CROSSTRAINING: To the classic exercise physiologist, crosstraining or crosseducation (they are synonymous) is a dynamogenic effect that results from exercising one body part while keeping the other inactive. The stationary part shows a marked increase in strength. For example, if one leg is immobilized by a cast, exercising the other leg will increase the strength of the immobilized one. This crosstraining effect is seen only when the motor nerves leading to the inactive muscles are functioning.

Modern athletes have taken the notion of crosstraining and applied it to the sport of swim-bike-run, leading us to a new definition:

A method of exercise (more than a specific technique) in which the effects of exercising in one sport increase the strength and fitness capacities in another sport.

CROSS-STRESS: A method of applying training demands on the body that includes simultaneous multisport conditioning.

CUMULATIVE FATIGUE: The depletion of stored and blood-born

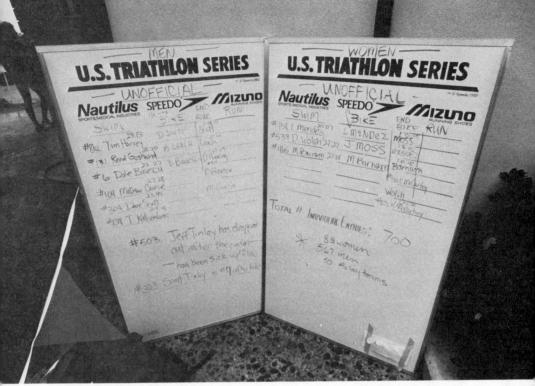

The first professional triathlon series began in the summer of 1982 with the initiation of the United States Triathlon Series (USTS), a five-city, West Coast production.

dietary fuels to each of the different muscle groups as they grow weary from athletic exertion, i.e. adding fuel losses from the swim stage to those from the bicycle stage, all of which cause a definite weakened condition at the start of the run stage.

(TO) IRON: The act of participating in the iron division. In a triathlon, the triathlete either relays or participates in the iron division.

IRONMAN (OR IRONWOMAN): A triathlete who competes in all three events (as opposed to a relay participant).

MET: A metabolic unit. One MET represents the amount of energy needed for a human being to function at rest and is related to oxygen consumption and metabolism. It can be used as a way to measure your fitness at any given time in an aerobic sport. (See Chapter 6)

MONITOR: A traffic controller.

MULTISPORT EVENT: An athletic contest that includes two or more activities in a particular sequence.

N.B.: *Note Bene,* Latin term meaning note well or pay close attention.

RACE DISTANCES: Today, there are no standard or accepted distances for triathlons, as there are in running, swimming, and cycling. There are different ways of defining the distance of the race according to the time span of the events:

1. *Standard triathlon*—a triple-event activity whose top contestants complete the entire race in less than two hours. Also called a *sprint triathlon.*

2. *Long-distance triathlon*—a triple-event race in which the contenders finish the race within two to four hours. Also called a *marathon triathlon.*

3. *Ultradistance triathlon*—a three-part, continuous event which the first finishers require more than four hours to complete. Also called an *ultratriathlon.*

SINGLE-SPORT SPECIALIST: An athlete who concentrates on only one event and, as a result, adapts to only one sport.

SPORT-SPECIFIC ACTIVITY: Physical activity that is directed toward one event in order to improve performance solely in that event. Training is based on the concept that the athlete must train only in one sport in order to become better at that sport.

STAGE: The individual activity within a multi-sport event.

TIN(MAN OR TINWOMAN): A slang term for a triathlete who participates in a short-course triathlon. Some consider tin(wo)men to be those who compete in distances less than Hawaii's long-course race. Others consider *tin(wo)man* a degrading term, as it suggests that races shorter than ultradistance are beneath true athletes.

TRANSITION: The time period in a triathlon race between the swim, bike, and run portions of the race.

TRANSITION AREA: The place where triathletes switch from one stage to another.

TRIAEROBICS: The activity of triple fitness under steady-state conditions with respect to the body's use of oxygen.

TRIATHLETE: A person trained or training for triple fitness or triathlon races requiring physical strength, skill, stamina, speed. A triathlete can approach the sport in one of four ways:

1. The *contender* plans, and has the ability, to place consistently among the top finishers.

2. The *strong finisher* does not intend to win or place high but wants to run the race to the best of his or her ability. Strong finishers train diligently and race hard but don't have the natural gifts necessary to win.

3. The *recreationalist* is the triathlete who loves to swim, bike, and run and to stay totally fit. Recreationalists may never race or may only occasionally enter a competition. Their motivation is the sheer joy, health, and fun of being fit.

4. The *survivalist* perceives triathlons as just another challenge. This is the "hero" who wants to tell the folks back home that he or she "did it." The survivalist has no real interest in the sport or in fitness; triathlons are merely ego-boosting activities.

TRIATHLETIC: The type of muscular, powerful, agile physique typical of a triathlete; an adjective referring to the sport.

TRIATHLETICISM: Adherence to, addiction to, or passion for triple fitness, or the quality of whole-body aerobic fitness.

TRIATHLETICS: The sport of triathlons.

TRIATHLOID: One who prefers to survive triathlons rather than train for them.

Three triathletes survey the swim course in preparation for that leg of the USTS race in San Diego.

TRIATHLOID CRAWL: Crossing the triathlon finish line on all fours (hands and knees) due to the inability to maintain an upright posture. The ultimate athletic insult as the triathloid is reduced to this incapacitated condition.

TRIATHLON: Any event that combines swimming, bicycling, and running.

TRIATHLON: An athletic contest in which each contestant takes part in three events. The triathletic contest can be either a *continuous event triathlon,* or a *stage-event triathlon,* in which each sport has a separate start and finish time, possibly on separate days. The contest can be an *iron division,* in which the contestants complete all three events by themselves, or a *relay division,* in which three different athletes combine to form a triathlon team. The most common and generally accepted definition of a triathlon includes the three sports—swim, bike, run—in that order.

TRI'ED: The past tense of the verb "to triathlon."

TRI-ING: The activity of participating in triathlons.

TRIPLE FITNESS: The condition of being in shape for three different sports simultaneously.

TRITRAINING: A workout program that incorporates three different fitness programs—specifically, swim-bike-run. Synonymous with *crosstraining.*

UNITED STATES TRIATHLON ASSOCIATION (USTA): The governing body of the sport of triathlons in the United States that is currently organizing the international body for the sport in order for the event to be accepted by the Olympic Games. The USTA registers athletes, sanctions and certifies races, lobbies for the sport, sets championships, and provides information to the public on the subject. For further information, contact USTA, P.O. Box 7708, Burbank, CA 91510; (213) 483-6181.

WALKING THE STATIONS: A triathlon dance step that allows the athlete to walk through aid stations.

WHOLE-BODY AEROBICS: Any vigorous exercise in which the uptake and utilization of oxygen are sufficient to meet the needs of the working muscles of the entire body. Examples of sports that improve oxygen intake and thus condition the heart and lungs are swimming, bicycling, running, rowing, and cross-country skiing.

training for triathlons: the aerobic 10 commandments

"Fitness is much more than just our physical bodies. Bodies are reflections of our inner selves. Put yourself in front of your own mental mirror and ask the question, "What do you want from life? What are your goals and desires?"

The annual Hawaii Ironman World Triathlon is a test for the whole body: 2½ miles of swimming in the ocean, 112 miles of bicycling across steaming lava beds, followed by 26.2 miles of running over the same course, all without pause between events. John Howard, a champion cyclist, was the men's 1981 International Triathlon winner. At the end of his race he stated that such ultradistance contests should be called *gruelathons*. The mileage is extreme; the temperatures are extreme; the competition is extreme; the time from start to finish is extreme. This 141-mile event taxes all systems to their speed and endurance limits. A top finisher must keep up a fast pace for many hours with no chance of rest. Each performance counts, from swimming to bicycling to running.

In Hawaii the marathon is the last event. The runner enjoys the least advantage of any specialist turned triathlete. Swimmers plunge into the ocean fresh at the start. Bicyclists mount their machines

Triathlons are growing with such mass participation as illustrated by the start of one of the USTS series races.

with legs still strong. The runner, however, steps forth with a severe handicap—no more juice. You might think that the experienced marathoner knows how to "hit the wall" afoot and survive. Yet when you hit the wall with 20 miles to go, psychological advantages soon dwindle. I was the third woman to finish the 1982 race. People ask me with a mixture of disbelief and curiosity, "How did you do it?"

The hard way, that's how! Until now no concise information has been available on how to train concurrently for three different events. The available sports training literature focuses individually on swimming, cycling, or running, not on all three combined. In Hawaii I could have done better if I had known better.

Triathlons are growing rapidly in popularity, attracting talented athletes from different specialties. Most triathlons are of a much more reasonable length than Hawaii's ultradistance race. Anyone reaching for high performance in multisport events will have to reach with the whole body; the properly conditioned triathlete is an all-around aerobic superstar. Such a star can exercise aerobically—in a steady, efficient, oxygen-using state—for long periods.

On the basis of race experience, research, and reacquaintance with my field of study, exercise physiology, I have developed an aerobic ten commandments for triathlon training. I offer them with something less than the authority of Moses, since the sport is still in the experimental stage.

Let's make some assumptions about you, the reader. You are probably a single-sport athlete—a runner, a swimmer, or a cyclist. You know how to swim the freestyle, ride a bicycle, and run a few miles at a reasonable pace. You probably are not very proficient at two of these three, but you like one of them so much that you define yourself socially as that type of athlete. You wish to try your hand at a new sport, and you are curious about the triathlon because it is challenging and new. You still love your primary sport, though, and are hesitant to commit to triathlon crosstraining because diversifying in three activities will take time away from your favorite and might reduce your peak in that sport.

That's where I started. I could barely swim, had never heard of James Councilman, and wasn't sure what Campagnola meant, but I could quote George Sheehan, chapter and verse. I loathed cold water and considered bicycling a real pain. Nonetheless, I was curious about how I might perform in a triathlon. So, without swimming a lap or riding my bicycle a mile in training, I entered one—a little one.

Sure enough, I did well in the first event—"my sport"—the run. But when the good bicyclists caught up and whizzed by on the second leg I sensed that I was out of my element. I knew for sure when I entered the cold lake swim for the third event. I did not finish *(DNF* is the athletic equivalent of *RIP)*. Embarrassed and disappointed, I decided there might be something to training and technique; simple luck and talent would not cut it.

With more determination than logic, I decided to race the biggest triathlon of them all and to train for a good performance. A swim coach taught me the fundamentals of the freestyle, breaking bad habits ingrained from lessons taken when I was 5 years old. A friend loaned me his fancy French 10-speed with his blessings and a few instructions. I climbed aboard this bright red, oversized LeJeune racing bicycle; and it responded like a champion breed. Kailua-Kona, watch out!

I had the basic tools of the trade in hand: membership in the local YMCA for swimming and weight training; a racing bicycle with helmet, shoes, gloves, and spare parts; and my beloved Nikes. Next I devised a training system that I thought would prepare me for Hawaii: I would swim five miles, run 50 miles, and cycle 100 miles per week for four months. That was the whole plan, period. Occasionally I followed it. I gave no thought to building strength and endurance; I had complete confidence that I could actually follow such a simplistic plan.

My training months did not go well that year, mostly because I lacked experience and confidence in my new events. None of my friends were cyclists. I rode alone or simply skipped workouts for lack of discipline, using the inclement winter weather as an excuse. The swimming phase posed different difficulties. The pools near me were available for lap swims only at hours I found inconvenient. Leaky goggles and crowded lanes added to the bother. Swimming requires tremendous concentration on technique and long, seemingly boring hours in the pool. Because my habits in cycling and swimming were not well-developed, the quality of my workouts was marginal. Of course, I was always looking for an excuse to skip a workout in my weak sports and slip out for a comfortable run instead.

In order to test training effectiveness, a friend and business partner and I decided to undertake a leisurely half-triathlon. All went well until her knee collapsed during the run; our confidence was shaken. A week later, we tested the individual events at full race distances, one event per day for three consecutive days. First, a three-mile pool swim—no stopping. I stopped anyway, using any excuse I could think of, and finished in an hour and 45 minutes—dizzy, bored, eyes blurred from chlorine. The next day we rode our bikes 100 miles point to point in a rainstorm with 30 mile-per-hour tail winds, which took just over five hours to finish, thanks to the push

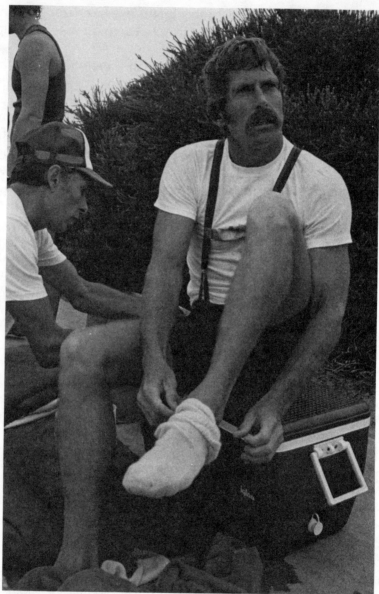

Tom Warren, considered the granddaddy of triathletes (1979 IRONMAN winner), contemplates the cycling stage of the race.

from behind. The marathon was so familiar and comfortable that I ran and walked the distance with ease on the third day.

The test was a good one. It exposed weaknesses in my conditioning and acquainted me with the race. But the training program as a whole was inadequate; I completed the actual race more on guts than on preparation.

Therefore, a change in my training was necessary. So the second year I trained systematically for Hawaii's ultradistance race and expected to do better. My program was based on a few sound scientific principles that are universally valid for aerobic endurance sports. These principles are not secrets of the trade. They are not formulas or gimmicks that will clip hours off your time; nor are they aphrodisiacs that will make you love your weakest sport. Instead they are physical fitness principles, or "commandments," that, if you adhere to them, will help lead you to successful endurance performance. In your specialty event, you probably take these principles for granted; yet, with new multisport athletic endeavor, you must learn to train for triple fitness.

COMMANDMENT #1:
Thou shalt aim neither too low nor too high.
PRINCIPLE:
Realistic Goals

Most athletes are encouraged to believe that overreaching will make dreams come true. Realism, however, is the requirement for maintaining steady progress. Many coaches insist that only an all-out commitment to suffering will win the race. They say, "If you are not willing to pay that price, don't play the game." Nonsense. Rather, set incremental goals that are progressively attainable. As you steadily build your abilities in new sports, you will feel satisfaction—even joy—rather than frustration.

When you have been in training for a while you will have a much clearer perception of who you are and where you want to go. These are the times when you need to readjust your goals, to reset your sights. It's OK to alter those goals—the review process is one that applies to both your daily workouts and your long-term assessment of your fitness. That is where the realism comes in—add the experience to the dreams, and you've hitched your wagon to the stars.

COMMANDMENT #2:
Thou shalt maintain continuity and discipline.
PRINCIPLE:
Good Habits

All your resolutions about hours, mileage, coaching, and races are useless unless you methodically chart out a program and monitor your progress. If it is true that "the road to hell is paved with good intentions," then run on firm footing. It is easy to expound on the miles of training that you intend to do, quite another to follow through with those good intentions. Habits are developed through practice. From the beginning, develop a triathlon frame of mind. Exercise regularly in all three sports, but focus on your weakest sport. Set aside regular hours for training and establish a daily/weekly/monthly routine that will consider all of the attendant, time-consuming rituals of dressing, warming up, and showering. Keep a training log and emphasize a disciplined nutrition program. Fitness in a sport slackens quickly when it is neglected.

COMMANDMENT #3:
Thou shalt neither sacrifice everything nor sacrifice nothing.
PRINCIPLE:
Balanced Values

Training requires time, which must be taken from other activities. It also requires money, sweat, and mental concentration. Your love may be running, yet you will have to cut back on running in order to train for your least favorite activity. In time, the slight sacrifice pays off. Triathlon training requires us to balance competing values and interests.

One of the most obvious conflicting values is the use of time, precious time. Your ability to budget the use of your time will make a key difference in juggling the other components of your triple-fitness lifestyle.

COMMANDMENT #4:
Thou shalt expand thy limits.
PRINCIPLE:
Demand and Overload

Research clearly demonstrates that you must stress your body beyond comfort in order to improve your aerobic fitness level.

Only when you make truly challenging demands on your various energy-restoring metabolic processes does your training become truly effective. Creating these demands is the *overload principle.* These demands must be of sufficient intensity to cause the body to adapt, to change. Even more important, the demands must not be greater than your present conditioning level allows—decrements in performance and injury will result from asking too much of your body. The flip side of the coin is that if you do not place sufficient demands on yourself, no improvement will occur.

After overloading your metabolic processes for several days/weeks you will feel a sensation of reduced effort; the same workout that was difficult before is now easier. This is the body's signal that you are adapting to overload—that your ability to perform (actually to replace energy and remove waste products) has improved. Pay attention to this. It means that you are no longer placing enough demands to push you into the overload zone. In order to continue to improve, you need to follow the *principle of progression*—to increase your training intensity continually so that you overload the appropriate metabolic processes.

For example, swimmers increase the speed of their intervals as the season progresses. At the beginning they might be swimming five sets of 100-yard sprints, each in two minutes. Later in the season they might swim each one in a minute and 45 seconds. In weight training, lifters increase the number of repetitions of a particular exercise (say, a bench press) systematically with each training session until they reach a predetermined goal. At that point they increase the weight and begin again at the original number of repetitions. Overloading can be of two types: either you can overload the intensity (or speed) of the workload or you can overload the endurance (or distance) of the workload. For example, you can run a given distance faster or run a greater distance at the same speed. Clearly, systematically increasing the intensity of your training—the definition of *interval training*—is the most effective method for progressive overloading.

In your new sports you have to make yourself hurt all over again.

COMMANDMENT #5:
Thou shalt progress in alternating hard–easy stages.
PRINCIPLE:
Stress and Recuperation

Work too hard or too long and you tear down both your body and your resolve. Work too easily and you waste your time. Between these extremes is an optimum point at which training effort produces maximum improvement, until eventually your muscles need a rest. It is difficult to know where this point is. Finding your body's balance requires careful monitoring.

The concept of rest is twofold. *Endurance rest* refers to continuing your workout program at a relaxed pace, say an easy three to five miles if your long-run day calls for 20 miles. *Strength rest*, though, refers to *absolute* rest. If you exercise a muscle group to the point of fatigue, through resistance (weight) training, for example, you must skip a day before you exercise again. An increase in muscle strength can take place only if the muscle group is allowed to rest in this way. See the chart on page 45 for an illustration of this principle as it applies to strength rest.

How do you continue to get stronger as your body cycles through stress and recuperation? The answer: monitor your pain. Push until you hurt and then pull back before you are injured. Go hard, then take it easy. Go long, then short. *Hurt* is a subjective condition. What constitutes hurt for me doesn't necessarily apply to you.

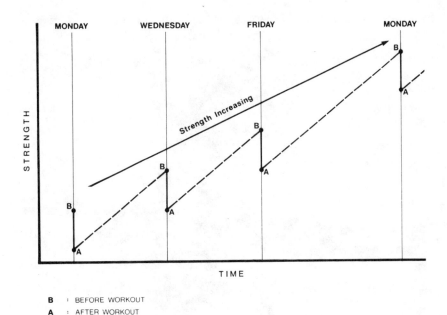

B   : BEFORE WORKOUT
A   : AFTER WORKOUT
— — : RECOVERY PERIOD

Muscle Recovery Patterns Before and After Alternate Day Workouts.

Hurting is a condition that requires that you be cautious and pay attention to your body. Certain kinds of pains act like a stoplight; they require that you stop exercising. Other kinds of hurt are possible to train through. Learn to tell the difference and train with that information in mind.

Here is a good test: You might begin a bicycle ride to find an ache in your right calf muscle. One of three things can happen—it can go away during the ride; it can continue but not get worse; it can get worse. In the first case you can probably train through the ache; in the second case, you might be able to; in the third you had better stop exercising. The physical and mental change of pace required by simultaneously staging stress-recovery in three sports will sharpen your interest and give rapid results. Remember, pain is the warning. Injury is the punishment.

If you are not having fun, you are not living.

This concept leads to the hard day–easy day training principle. One day you will stress yourself by placing progressively increasing demands on your strength-endurance adaptation processes. The next day you need to ease up on the throttle, relax, and allow your body to recuperate so that it can be rested and ready for the next demand.

Soon, exercise physiologists will be able to tell us, based on their studies, whether we can cross-stress our daily workouts; that is, whether we can, for example, consecutively swim hard, cycle easy, and run hard.

Right now, because of the lack of hard data, each of us must find out what works best for us through self-experimentation; that's part of the excitement of the triple-training program.

COMMANDMENT #6:
Thou shalt receive only what thou workest for.
PRINCIPLE:
Specificity

At first this may be one of the more difficult commandments to accept. We often ask ourselves whether there is a carry-over effect from one sports activity to another. For example, since bicycling and running both improve aerobic fitness, if you do one sport regularly, shouldn't you also become proficient in the other? On the contrary, available research suggests that conditioning programs must be directed specifically at the sport in which you are training. Thus, it is important to crosstrain specifically in all three sports of the triathlon.

If you insist on boasting, "I'm in shape," you must be prepared to answer the question, "For what?" Are you in shape just to run or are you in triple shape? This concept of sport-specific training is based on the fact that muscles adapt to the particular demand placed on the metabolic processes in a specific way. To train your leg extensors (quadriceps) to endure hours of spinning, you must spend hours spinning. An extension of this principle is that the body also learns specificity with regard to speed. If you run slowly, your body will specifically train itself to run slowly. You will be a slow runner. Conversely, if you train fast, your metabolic processes will adapt to the speed, and you will run fast. Finally, if you apply the principle of specificity to training the anaerobic threshold, you will discover that you can improve the rate of waste product removal from the exercised muscle groups. That is, you can extend the onset of fatigue by training at intensities that are slightly in excess of your present level of anaerobic threshold.

COMMANDMENT #7:
Thou shalt lose what thou dost not use.
PRINCIPLE:
Regression

Fitness is lost rapidly when it is not maintained through frequent workouts of adequate distance and intensity. After three or four days of inactivity you have to climb back to where you were, and regaining fitness is harder than maintaining fitness.

This is the disuse principle. If you don't use it, you will lose it. If you don't progressively strengthen or maintain your fitness level, it will atrophy, and the functional size of the muscle groups will decrease. Your muscles will become weaker, and you will lose muscle tone. This condition begins after three days of inactivity. Clearly, the triathlete can afford to wallow in this condition only when it results from overtraining or injury—both regressive conditions.

COMMANDMENT #8:
Thy goal shall be thy life.
PRINCIPLE:
Preparation

Prepare yourself mentally by reading every pertinent article or book. Prepare yourself physically by following a well-planned training schedule. Prepare yourself emotionally by pushing the limit of your endurance. Prepare yourself psychologically by progressing to ever higher goals. To be an athlete in spirit as well as in deed

Through the exploration, through the experience, we learn that it takes more than the bike, the Nikes, the muscles—it takes the help of friends.

you must organize your life around your objective. Training for triathlons is a lifestyle.

What greater goal can you have in your life than to become more physically, mentally, and spiritually fit every year? The triathlon lifestyle blends into this formula for whole-body fitness. It is the foundation of all mental and spiritual health.

COMMANDMENT #9:
Thou must know the race to perform the race well.
PRINCIPLE:
Testing

Measure your progress in training by testing yourself at full-race distances in each event. You should dry-run a minitriathlon before actually entering competition. As a result you will perform even better in the race. Being pumped up for the race is not enough; adrenaline and desire will not compensate for poor preparation.

One of the reasons that people play the triathlon sport is that it offers them an opportunity to test their whole-body aerobic fitness. But this testing is more than measurement, analysis of fitness, a test of cans and cannots. Rather, one of the appeals of the triathlon test is to find the pathway that leads back to yourself. George Sheehan, the running philosopher, has said that intense physical activity is necessary for us to become "good animals." We learn who we are by combining our experiences with our genetic inheritance, and growth comes from the combination of life and reflection on that experience. The triathlon provides the variety of athletic experiences that allows us to develop ourselves and expand our knowledge of ourselves.

COMMANDMENT #10:
Thou shalt enjoy thine ordeal.
PRINCIPLE:
Play and Variety

Keep your mind busy by planning and logging your training experience. With rhythmic building in three separate sports, each day will be refreshingly unique. Triathlon training is an individual experiment that heightens the communication between brain and body. You'll be outdoors much of each day in all kinds of weather, and you'll travel many different routes. If you are not having fun, *you are not living.*

The rigors and requirements of whole-body triple fitness can be felt only if they are balanced with that ingredient of fitness—fun. If you look back to your triathlon roots, as children we were romping on the triathlon playground for pure, unadulterated fun. That is what the triathlon will do—take you back to your childhood and reawaken your spirit of youth and vitality.

COMMANDMENT #11:
Thou shalt discover thine own commandments.
PRINCIPLE:
Exploration and Discovery

The sport of triathlon is in its infancy. Its popularity in America is just beginning; the electronic media and fitness-conscious participants are just starting to become aware of the triathlon's potential. And there's a lot more to come.

As incipient triathletes, you are the pioneers of the sport. You are the explorers of its untested grounds and waters—learning through the school of experience about training, racing, lifestyle, and budgeting time. You have made the transition from a single-sport specialty and are breaking ground for those who come after you.

Explore and discover!

5

the measure of madness: a self-analyzing test

"The reason that we do this is to further extend our frontiers."

Any runner looking 26.2 miles down the road from the starting line is asking a question the next few hours will answer. The same is true of a 100-mile bicycle racer, an endurance swimmer, and a triathlete performing all three events in succession. Both the question posed and the answer provided are unique to the individual. A private ordeal—a personal triumph meeting the challenge of sport—is a test of the will.

And it's a test of the "won't." The human body is more than an instrument of the mind's intentions. Physical and psychic life exist in collaboration for the athlete—the body complains of its limitations to the mind, and the mind responds with its ambitions to the body. In endurance sports, of the two, the body is wiser. But the mind rules like an imperious warrior conquering new truths in pursuit of a vision. Wisdom is along for the ride, until it proclaims that the ride is over.

A triathlete may have to peer as far as 141 miles to see that finish banner in the distance, with two other banners in between. What kind of will and what kind of wisdom together enable a competitor first to train for and then to race a heroic swim, plus a century cycle, plus a marathon run?

In Hawaii's International Triathlon, an ultradistance race, such consecutive distances are an excruciating fact. The sport is luring new devotees with an elite metallurgical status withheld from other endurance-sport specialists—the title *Ironperson*. The titles *Ironwoman* and *Ironman* suggest the kind of colossal invincibility usually reserved for comic book superheroes, a bit of swagger to accompany the stagger after 141 miles of muscle propulsion.

The stuff of daydreams, yes? Maybe just your sort of mad, adventurous challenge. If so, you might first take the measure of your madness before plunging, pedaling, and pounding onward toward your goal. Are you a champion or just the breakfast of champions? Time to take stock. Stand before a mirror and look eye to eye with your self-image. You are about to give yourself— warrior mind and wise-man body—the triathlon quiz:

SELF ANALYZING YOUR TRIATHLON POTENTIAL

Answer each question *Yes, No,* or *Not sure.*

1. **DO YOU KNOW YOUR PERSONAL STYLE FOR ESTABLISHING AND WORKING TOWARD GOALS?** Some people are hardheaded straight-line strivers, and some are sail-with-the-wind strivers. There are innumerable ways to aim for accomplishment. Whatever your own style as a triathlete, it must be purposeful rather than aimless. *Answer:* _____

2. **CAN YOU LAY OUT YOUR PRESENT SCHEDULE AND EITHER FIND OR CREATE TIME?** Time is available for what must be done. With ingenuity you might train while bike commuting and swim on your lunch hour. Athletic training is a matter of managing time and avoiding lost opportunities. It is a matter of budgeting time. *Answer:* _____

Scott Tinley is the only man to finish in the top three places in the last three years.

3. **CAN YOU ADAPT TO CHANGE AND ACCOMMODATE THE UNFORESEEN?** A triathlete may have three times the chance for unwanted surprises—illness, injury, demands from job or family. You can take all hurdles in stride if you are a patient, careful planner rather than an easily frustrated, overly demanding person.
   Answer: _____

4. **CAN YOU DISPENSE WITH SELF-PUNISHING GUILT AND SEE TRAINING AS A FLOWING PROCESS, NOT AS SOMETHING THAT'S EITHER BUILT UP OR DESTROYED EASILY, LIKE A FRAGILE TOWER OF CARDS?** Some people set themselves up for failure by ignoring their successes— the "you're not doing well enough" syndrome. Any deviation from schedule or failure to meet expectations is regarded as a cardinal sin, as if being tough on oneself will soften any disapproval from on high. A successful triathlete takes pride in progress, learns from difficulties and lives the lifestyle.
   Answer: _____

5. **CAN YOU BALANCE OTHER COMPETING VALUES AND COMPROMISE WHEN FACING DIVERSE DEMANDS WITHOUT ABANDONING SOMETHING DEAR TO YOUR LIFE?** A dedicated triathlete keeps all facets of life in balanced perspective, knowing that psychological health is as important to performance as is physical health. Happiness is the whole cookie, not just a crumb. A triathlete must be humanistic (e.g., one who shares balanced concerns for others) rather than obsessive (e.g., egocentric).
   Answer: _____

6.. **CAN YOU SHARE YOUR COMMITMENT WITH LOVED ONES BY INVITING THEM INTO YOUR VISION?** The people who care about you want to help. In nutrition, recreation, and education, find ways to bring your loved ones into the picture. Share your interests creatively; avoid selfish isolation. Program your crosstraining lifestyle so that it includes sharing with others.
   Answer: _____

7. **CAN YOU RECOGNIZE TRUTH AND AVOID FOOLING YOURSELF?** The body is ever honest and is ready to give its life in loyal service to the will. A fool dismisses the body's grievances about overtraining, poor nutrition, injury, and illness. At the other extreme, the fool also thinks the body is somehow easily capable of what it has not been conditioned to do. In sport, as in love, desire can overwhelm good sense unless you are relentlessly honest.
   Answer: _____

8. **CAN YOU DELAY ULTIMATE GRATIFICATION BY SAVORING SMALL PLEASURES ON THE WAY TO ACHIEVING BIG ONES?** Training is a process; performance, a product. A wise triathlete finds day-to-day rewards in the preparation itself. You might even come to prefer training over the actual race for the feelings of fitness and the outdoor

"What do you mean they lost my swim suit?"

adventures that continual training provides. Like the old prospector in wild country, you need not find gold to make the search worthwhile. Appreciate the beauty of the search. Remember, the fun is in the traveling, not necessarily in the arrival.
Answer: _____

9. **CAN YOU FOLLOW YOUR INTENTIONS, KEEP IN STEP WITH YOUR OWN RHYTHMS, AND IGNORE INAPPRO-PRIATE ADVICE OR GAMESMANSHIP?** Some athletes think they are in competition right from the first day of training. If someone else is doing triple workouts daily, then they have to do likewise. Keeping secrets about training, technique, or nutrition gives the illusion of a competitive edge. What seems to be working for someone else may not work for you. Be inner-directed rather than outer-distracted; look inward and listen to yourself.
Answer: _____

10. **WHEN A SETBACK OCCURS, CAN YOU ACCEPT RESPONSIBILITY FOR INITIATING REMEDIAL ACTION, KNOWING THAT NO MATTER WHAT GOT YOU INTO A FIX, YOU HAVE TO GET YOURSELF OUT?** In athletics, as in the rest of life, when something goes wrong the inclination to blame oneself or others often rears its warty head. Learning from experience is wise, but either vilifying or vindicating history is a silly waste of brain power. Tackle your future; don't haggle over the past.
Answer: _____

11. **CAN YOU DELIBERATELY APPROACH PAIN AGAIN AND AGAIN, YET RESPOND REPEATEDLY TO ITS WARNING BY BACKING OFF, EVEN LAYING OFF?** The aphorism "No pain, no gain" is not a license for masochism. Some athletes dote on self-torture by continually pushing themselves to the breaking point, then suffering the consequences, some even with satisfaction. Others cry out at every twinge of pain

It is a happy triathlete that knows how to play.

like hyperhypochondriacs. Many competitive athletes dread taking off any time, as if in one day of rest all that they have worked for will collapse. Is this the Puritan work ethic or is it paranoia? Nudging the pain threshold upward, then resting after overload is the only way to gain strength and endurance. A mature triathlete is objective rather than passionate about pain, neither loving nor fearing it—just using it.

Answer: _____

12. **CAN YOU CLAIM HIGH-LEVEL FITNESS IN AT LEAST ONE AEROBIC ENDURANCE SPORT?** Your cardiovascular system is basic gear for swimming, cycling, and running. Your muscle sets for unfamiliar movement inevitably will need conditioning, but your heart and lungs should need no significant upgrading. If you call yourself a runner and

They come from all walks of life.

a seven-minute mile seems like a sprint, or if you are primarily a cyclist who can't break two hours for 25 miles, or if you are first and foremost a swimmer who fatigues severely after half a mile in the pool, then your specialty is not aerobically strong. Of course, you may be able to complete a long triathlon by taking all events at a slow but steady pace, which is a worthy accomplishment. Just be realistic rather than romantic about how hard you can push for a top performance.

Answer: _____

13. CAN YOU READILY LEARN NEW PHYSICAL SKILLS AND MAINTAIN GOOD FORM EVEN WHEN YOU ARE FATIGUED? If you are mastering new sports, you need adaptable motor abilities, including balance, coordination, kinesthetic sense, and quickness. Athletic adjustability is only partly a matter of genetic inheritance. More important is the confidence gained and then sustained through sensitive teaching, especially when you have to be your own teacher. Develop the habit of self-visualization—seeing yourself in the process of training as if through a camera lens, then feeling for what you see to confirm your vision. In this way you can get the most out of what little energy you have left near the end of a race. Skill counts most when power is at its weakest.

Answer: _____

End of quiz. No points to score, no grade to award. The test is intended to start a learning process—learning about yourself.

If you don't score yourself as one who wants to compete in a triathlon, that's fine. The fitness benefits of tritraining are unquestionably valuable. By definition you are an athlete—a triathlete—if you participate.

How about age, sex, and handicaps—the kind of data requested on standard physical exams? As the lawyers on television shows say, irrelevant, immaterial, and inadmissible. In the Hawaii Ironman Triathlon, women left many of the men behind, a blind athlete went the full distance, and Walt Stack, age 74, completed the race in 26 hours and 20 minutes.

Triathlons, you see, are an equal opportunity insanity.

6

testing for performance

"The ancient Greeks considered fitness, health, and beauty among the most admirable of human traits. For modern mortals, there is crosstraining, the true fitness program for those who take to heart the ideal of the well-rounded human being."

The idea of attempting a triathlon has excited your imagination, but you are wondering how to start. Remember the beginning of your athletic career in swimming, cycling, or running? If only you knew then what you know now, you could have avoided the trial-and-error pitfalls of your early days. You might never have started, but that's another story.

You can put your hard-won wisdom to work by applying old lessons to this new sport. The method for success has been utilized by generations of athletes. It goes like this:

Step 1: Find out what your present level of conditioning is.

Step 2: Take a psychological inventory.

Step 3: Set some goals and chart a course of travel based on this information—a training program.

Step 4: Periodically test your progress.

Step 5: Modify the training program as you analyze the results.

This is the way to gain fitness in a logical fashion. The step-by-step method lets you create your powers out of your own potential. You need not compare your determination, your skills, or your aerobic capacity to anyone else's. The responsibility is on your shoulders; the laurels will rest on your brow.

The first and fourth steps require a method for self-testing: assessing your present physical condition. You need methods to assess, in the field, your current fitness to cycle, swim, and run. There *is* a way to analyze your conditioning level in each of the three sports without going to a human performance lab. These methods are simple tests that express your ability to race against the clock in terms of your present aerobic capacity.

METS

When a person is at rest, the amount of energy (or number of calories) being used in one minute can be expressed as one met, or one metabolic unit. This is the energy required by the body to carry out the basic functions of life; e.g., maintaining body temperature, pumping blood, digesting food, and performing other functions. Since individual body sizes vary considerably, it seems obvious that different people would require different amounts of energy at rest to maintain life.

The concept of the met takes these differences into account. At rest, each of us takes in (breathes) between 3.5 and 4.0 milliliters (ml) of oxygen (O_2) per kilogram of body weight per minute (min). A met, therefore, is a standardized unit. Differences in body weight (kg) between me and you are built into the formula (1 met = 3.5–4.0 ml O_2/kg/min), because the purpose of mets is not to compare one person to another, but rather *to compare the energy (oxygen-burning) demands of one level of intensity of activity to that of another* for the same person.

One's oxygen uptake (the amount necessary to handle a given work load, measured in liters per minute) is a sure indicator of aerobic-power output, because all body fuels need oxygen to burn metabolically. The demand due to any exertion above rest can be

Dave Scott, after winning a USTS race, smiles because he passed the self-test—he is getting better.

expressed as a multiple of the uptake at rest or as multiple mets. If a certain amount of work requires 70 milliliters of oxygen per kilogram of your weight in one minute, then that power requirement would equal 20 mets:

$$\frac{70 \text{ ml O}_2}{3.5 \text{ ml O}_2/\text{kg/min}} = 20 \text{ mets}$$

Performance times can be correlated with metabolic power output (expressed in multiples of mets). Using your elapsed time at a specific distance gives us a good ball-park method of estimating your aerobic capacities in different sports.

Each sport—running, biking, and swimming—places a specific

metabolic demand on you at your top speed in each. Because of training specificity, your "max mets" in the three tests may differ considerably. If you are an excellent runner and a poor swimmer, your test results express the contrast in terms of a common denominator—metabolic intensity. You already know that you can be competent in one sport and not in another. Now the concept of mets gives you a way to compare your levels of ability in different sports. To reiterate, if you are a swimmer, your mets level in that sport will probably be higher than it will for you in cycling because of your sport-specific training.

Prior to taking the self-tests for maximum mets, you should heed the standard warnings. If you are over the age of 35, I urge you to see your doctor (preferably a sportsmedicine physician) for a physical examination. The exam should include a stress electro-cardiogram because too many people with undiagnosed heart disease are taking part in conditioning programs. If you haven't been exercising in one or more of these three sports, start a conditioning program that progressively leads up to the distances. Don't go into these rigorous time trials cold. For best results, don't try more than one test per day.

1½-MILE RUN SELF-TEST

The purpose of the 1½-mile run test is to measure your present aerobic running capacity in mets. The distance is too long for an oxygen-debt sprint; you need your endurance to make it to the end. Running it at your top steady speed provides a measure of your current maximum aerobic metabolic rate. Before taking the test you should have been running at least five miles per week for six weeks or more. This is to insure that you have prepared yourself properly for the demand of the test.

Warm up thoroughly before taking the test. For some, this may mean stretching, walking, or light jogging to warm up the heart muscle as well as the legs. It's best to conduct the test on a 440-yard track (six laps). Run the fastest pace you can maintain for the full distance—you shouldn't have much energy left at the end. Measure

Table 1: 1½-Mile Run Self-Test*

Elapsed Time (min:sec)	Pace (min per mile)	Max Mets
8:05	5:22	18.0
8:20	5:33	17.5
8:35	5:43	17.0
8:55	5:56	16.5
9:10	6:06	16.0
9:31	6:20	15.5
9:50	6:33	15.0
10:16	6:50	14.5
10:35	7:10	14.0
11:01	7:20	13.5
11:31	7:40	13.0
12:01	8:00	12.5
12:35	8:23	12.0
13:10	8:46	11.5
13:50	9:13	11.0
14:31	9:40	10.5
15:20	10:13	10.0
16:10	10:46	9.5
17:16	11:30	9.0
18:25	12:16	8.5
19:40	13:06	8.0
21:16	14:10	7.5

*Adapted from Dr. Thomas D. Fahey's *The Good Time Fitness Book,* Butterick Publishing, 1978, with permission.

the elapsed time, then refer to Table 1, which will tell you your max mets; i.e., your present maximum metabolic capacity for running.

The 1½-mile run self-test is a good substitute for the treadmill test, which is the most accurate method of measurement. For most people the treadmill test is both expensive and not readily available for retesting during the conditioning program.

In your training progression you will periodically need to take the 1½-mile run self-test to measure improvement or the lack thereof. You will use this information to monitor your performance and determine when you need to increase the intensity and duration of your exercise.

In my triathlon training program I self-test once per week in one of the three sports. Because competitive running has been my specialty, my max mets test for the 1½-mile run has remained between 8:30 and 8:40 minutes, which places me at a 17.0 max mets level. Again, I place high because of my 15 years of running experience. Most new triathletes will initially score below the 13.0 max mets level and will be working to raise their level.

THREE-MILE BICYCLE SELF-TEST

By racing a three-mile time trial you can determine your current max mets for cycling. Your performance will be affected by factors in addition to conditioning—the fit and quality of the bicycle, the tire pressure, your body aerodynamics, etc. The met requirements in Table 2 were computed with a standard 10-speed rather than with a stationary bicycle ergometer, because wind resistance increases geometrically as you speed up. The faster you go, the more you buck your own head wind.

To prepare for this test, measure a flat, straight course with no obstructions, choose a windless day, warm up properly, and ride as fast as you can at a steady pace. Keep the stopwatch going to measure the total elapsed time during the test. Refer to Table 2 to compute the bicycle max mets.

400-YARD SWIM SELF-TEST

Because of individual differences in stroke efficiency, correla-

Table 2: Three-Mile Bicycle Self-Test*

Elapsed Time (min:sec)	Pace (miles per hour)	Max Mets
5:53	30.6	20.0
6:00	30.0	19.5
6:08	29.3	19.0
6:17	28.8	18.5
6:26	27.8	18.0
6:35	27.0	17.5
6:45	26.6	17.0
6:55	26.0	16.5
7:05	25.4	16.0
7:17	24.7	15.5
7:29	24.0	15.0
7:41	23.4	14.5
7:54	22.7	14.0
8:08	22.1	13.5
8:23	21.4	13.0
8:39	20.7	12.5
8:56	20.1	12.0
9:14	19.4	11.5
9:33	18.8	11.0
9:54	18.1	10.5
10:16	17.5	10.0
10:40	16.9	9.5
11:05	16.2	9.0
11:33	15.5	8.5
12:04	14.9	8.0
12:37	14.2	7.5
13:13	13.6	7.0
13:53	12.9	6.5
14:37	12.3	6.0
15:26	11.7	5.5
16:21	11.0	5.0

*Adapted from Dr. Thomas D. Fahey's *The Good Time Fitness Book,* Butterick Publishing, 1978, with permission.

Table 3: 400-Yard Swim Self-Test*

Elapsed Time (min:sec)	Pace (equivalent min/mile)	Max Mets
5:01	22:04	20.0
5:07	22.31	19.5
5:13	22:58	19.0
5:20	23:27	18.5
5:27	23:59	18.0
5:34	24:28	17.5
5:41	24:59	17.0
5:49	25:36	16.5
5:57	26:11	16.0
6:05	26:45	15.5
6:14	27:24	15.0
6:23	28:04	14.5
6:32	28:44	14.0
6:42	29:29	13.5
6:53	30:16	13.0
7:04	31:06	12.5
7:16	31:59	12.0
7:28	32:49	11.5
7:41	33:47	11.0
7:55	34:48	10.5
8.10	35.56	10.0
8:26	37:05	9.5
8:43	38:22	9.0
9:01	39:41	8.5
9:20	41:03	8.0
9:41	42:35	7.5
10:03	44:13	7.0
10:27	45:59	6.5
10:53	47:52	6.0
11:21	49:56	5.5
11:52	52:13	5.0
12:25	54:38	4.5
13:02	57:20	4.0

*Adapted from Dr. Thomas D. Fahey's The Good Time Fitness Book, Butterick Publishing, 1978, with permission.

tions between speed and energy output are inexact. A strong but slow swimmer with bad technique may expend as much energy thrashing through the water as a world-class swimmer who is setting a distance record.

Prepare for the swim by warming up properly. Choose a pool at least 25 yards long. You should be fit enough to swim continuously for 20–30 minutes without difficulty. Time yourself with a stopwatch or a wall clock and swim as powerfully as you can at a steady speed. Refer to Table 3 for the metabolic maximum for your performance.

As mentioned earlier, the better shape you are in for each individual sport, the higher your max mets. As a general rule of thumb, your max mets in each sport should be greater than 12 or 13, regardless of your age. If your max mets are less than 10, you will have to do a lot of work to improve both your skills and your aerobic capacity.

Design your workouts so that they demand the stress necessary to deliver improvements. Mix speed, distance, rest, play, power, cadence, strength, and flexibility into a training program that leads to a progressive improvement of your aerobic fitness.

MEASURING YOUR PROGRESS

Retake the max met self-tests at least once per month for each sport so that you can evaluate your progress. Write down the results in your training log. If you do not notice a change in your max mets after several months, then either you are maximally fit for the exercise program or a change in your training program is necessary to place the demands on you needed for improvement.

If you measure your max mets and determine that they have improved, the program is working.

Bear in mind that the tables in this chapter are intended only for your self-assessment in three distinct sports. They are not valid for making comparisons among individuals. Your rest metabolic rates may differ from mine as well as from the average met. The max met scale is a guide to help the triathlete judge relative strengths and weaknesses and relative improvements.

Since swimming is my weakest sport, in preparing for the 1982 triathlon racing season (April–October), I followed my own advice and self-tested in swimming once a week. I can remember the first time I took the 400-yard swim self-test and finished in 7 minutes, 50 seconds, for a score of 10.5 max mets. I was clearly embarrassed that I didn't score at least 12 max mets, so I worked harder; three weeks later I retested and scored 12.5 max mets. I was absolutely thrilled and called Carl Thomas, vice-president of Speedo International and my swimming confidant, just to tell him I was improving. (I'm sure he didn't completely understand my excitement.) The last time I tested myself I was above the 14-met mark, and I began to wonder if I could swim as strongly as I could run. Indeed, the training program I wrote to improve my weakest sport is working. That's one of the thrills of self-testing; you can enjoy the process of getting better.

beginning a triathlon training program

"It is more than the will to win; it is the will to train that counts."

In the last decade Americans by the millions have gotten serious about getting in shape, and the numbers of people genuinely committed to physical fitness and athletic excellence continue to grow. Likewise, the arguments over the best training systems grow—the best way to achieve your goals, the most efficient kind of workout, etc. Some people favor all-aerobic work (e.g., long-slow distance); others prefer to swim-bike-run shorter distances at a faster pace. Other triathletes alternate hard and easy workouts; still others prefer more uniformity in their training. Weight training is an integral part of some athletes' training routines; others don't know a rep from a set.

Proponents of each type cite the successful performances of one or more elite champions as evidence that their system is the best. These "experts" would have you believe that if you follow the training program of Allison Roe, John Marino, of Diana Nyad that you can achieve their levels of aerobic conditioning and success. It often seems simpler to copy another person's training program than to think through the problem and plan your own.

Fortunately, the controversy continues. What would we talk about if the debate were resolved, assuming that that is possible

Carl Thomas studies the women's race results.

in the first place? Part of the mystique of training is the uncertainty, the speculation and the superstition, the differences among systems. The reason for the apparent confusion and lack of uniformity is that, as George Sheehan has said, "Each person is an experiment of one." What works for one athlete, scholar, or nutritionist may not work for others.

How, then, do you design a training program that will make unique little you a big success? You can hire a coach or spend a lot of money on physiological testing, risking sweat and hope, hours and egos on the outcome and judgment of others. Or, with a little self-evaluation, you can design a training program based on *proper* planning.

There are general training principles that apply to everyone, but it's important to remember that it's a one-person, one-plan world. I know of no other athlete who follows the same program, eats the same diet, sleeps the same hours, or lives with the same stresses that I do. That is the nature of life; yet there are coaches and trainers who preach the "right way" to all their athletes, disregarding those individual differences that are as distinct as fingerprint patterns. When a "right way" works for a few among the many, a coach is lauded as the greatest—few notice those for whom the program doesn't work.

I know what works for me: a crosstraining program that fits into my life. The same will apply to you. You can plan a triple-fitness program whose details fit *your* life and avoid relying on luck or what is better suited to another's life. The training methods discussed here have evolved from 20 years of experience in competition and athletic coaching. I have used them to win footraces ranging from 10 kilometers to 100 miles. The underlying principles are the "secrets" that some athletic competitors keep to themselves, a combination of ideas from a variety of sources—physiologists, nutritionists, psychologists, and other athletes. This system has worked well for me, and some personalized variation of it will work for you.

Any triathlon training plan depends on the components of the specific contest—the order and distance of each segment in a given race. One training strategy is to strengthen your weakest sport and to emphasize the most demanding leg of the race. Each plan must look like the blueprint for a house designed by the person who will build it and live in it, a creation that requires self-awareness and intelligence.

SETTING GOALS

Before you can plan a training system you have to have specific goals in mind. These should be based on an inventory and self-analysis of your endurance base, fitness skills, and talents as a cyclist, swimmer, and runner. My primary goal, for example, is to improve my performance from that of the last race I've entered. I compare myself only with myself—my purpose is to train better and finish faster than before.

Your swim-bike-run goals should be expressed numerically, in terms of a specific pace per mile or a specific finishing time.

This makes it easier to plan day-to-day and month-to-month workouts and to monitor your progress. For example, if I want to improve on my marathon PR of 2:53, I might choose a goal of 2:49 as a finishing time. My training purpose, then, is to develop both an endurance base sufficient to maintain a fast pace over a long distance and a top aerobic speed much in excess of my pacing target.

You can revise the numerical or quantitative objectives upward as your training progresses. For example, in the early weeks of training I might target my interval work at a 5:50-per-mile pace, and I might aim for 20 miles at a seven-minute pace for distance work. Later I might be running sub-5:30 interval miles and be doing my distance work at close to race pace.

In triathlons, of course, you have three events for which to establish goals and objectives. If you've never entered a triathlon before, or if the distance of one or more of the segments of the triathlon is new to you, then you have no standards for comparison or goal setting. One approach you can take is to obtain a copy of the race splits (elapsed times of each individual segment of the race) from the previous year's race. From the splits you can see what kind of effort was necessary to finish in a particular position, in the middle of the pack or ahead of it. Then you can assess your present capabilities in swimming, cycling, and running and consider how much time you have to train—in terms of both hours in the day and months of the calendar. In other words, you can be realistic about whether it makes sense to enter a specific triathlon at all (i.e., whether you have sufficient time to prepare for the kind of performance you want to achieve) and what kind of training is necessary to get you there.

Since your training goals need to be aimed at specific triathlon distances, decide on the sprint, the marathon, or the ultratriathlon event. You will be writing your conditioning program based on this decision. If you are entering the sprint triathlon, you need to train at lower mileage and higher interval–type workouts. If you train for ultratriathlons, the reverse will be true: you'll do more long aerobic workouts and fewer workouts that incorporate anaerobic speed training.

For the February 1982 Ironman Triathlon in Hawaii, swimming at a 40-minute-per-mile pace, cycling at 17 miles-per-hour, and running at an 8½-minute-per-mile pace would have made you the third woman overall in a field of 58, with a total time of 11 hours and 50 minutes. Swimming at a 25-minute-per-mile pace, cycling at 22 miles-per-hour, and running a seven-minute-per-mile pace would have placed you first overall in nine hours and eight minutes, more than 11 minutes ahead of winner Scott Tinley.

I think it is realistic for women athletes who have the time to train to aim for the top spot. In their specialties women are performing well beyond the best triathlon splits overall, and women have the endurance capacities to excel at the cumulative distance. Some day the first Ironperson could be an Ironwoman!

While we're considering the matter of goals, don't overlook the matter of your ideal performing weight. This may not be a problem to world-class athletes who train and compete at high levels on a continuing basis. But if you're new to this business, take a good look at your body and remember how much extra energy it takes to haul superfluous poundage around. After all, what's the point of spending an extra $500 on a superlight bicycle if you more than make up for it in excess body weight? So, also make weight loss part of your crosstraining plan. You can do so one of two ways— either by decreasing your caloric intake or by increasing your training load (or by using a combination of the two). It probably doesn't make sense to try to lose more than a pound a week while you maintain your training, but this only amounts to eating 500 fewer calories per day.

HOW TO START

Before you can begin tritraining you must establish minimum proficiency in each of the three sports involved—swimming, bicycling, and running. You must be able to complete certain specific distances at a reasonable pace (which you determine). Those of you who are already proficient in the three sports can now skip ahead to the next chapter. Beginners, however, should pay close attention here.

The beginning moment is where you are now. What minimum standards do you want to set for proficiency? Set them yourself, for you are the only one who is familiar with your history of athletic experiences, your skill levels, and your interests. You need not follow these exact guidelines, but these distances will serve as minimum distances for our goals.

Swim—1 mile continuously
Bike—25 miles continuously
Run—5 miles continuously

Note that *crosstraining*—integrating three sports into a weekly conditioning program—is not our concern here. Rather, in this chapter we will explore the requirements for beginning training in each of three different sports, with the goal of becoming reasonably accomplished in each. Let's assume that you are at the starting point and need to know everything about heading down those seemingly endless lanes, with black stripes on each side!

SWIMMING GOAL: ONE MILE CONTINUOUSLY

I can remember that I made my long awaited return to the swimming pool with great trepidation. Knowing little about triathlons, I had decided to enter one "cold turkey." After a dismal experience I realized that I *could* excel at the sport with training— which required that I join a local swimming pool, in my case the YMCA. That first time I was like a baby bird on its first outing from the nest. I didn't know which direction to swim in the lane, that lanes were designated by pace, that a wall clock was used for intervals, that there were certain courtesies that are observed by lap swimmers. It wasn't until my second year of training that I

The look of confidence after finishing the swim stage.

mustered the courage to join the Masters swimmers. I hesitated initially because I felt that I was too inexperienced and that they wouldn't accept me. Such silly thoughts. Today I know that they seek out people such as myself who are hungry for information and improvement.

The key to beginning any aerobic conditioning program is to start slowly and increase gradually, adding bits of distances and pieces of time to the progression. Swimming smoothly and efficiently requires that you follow the triathlon tripod for fitness: talent, dedication, and technique.

Talent is what you are given to work with. Analyze your background. If you swam as a child, you will progress in this sport with greater ease than if you are new to the sport of aquatic endurance. To develop your talent, join a swim club, take some stroke lessons, subscribe to *SWIM SWIM* magazine, and introduce yourself to the people who practice aquatic fitness and competitive swimming. Learn the jargon so that you can slip into conversations on bilateral breathing, hypoxic training, bobbing, treading, and sculling. Invest in the equipment of the sport.

Dedication—the second leg of the triathlon tripod—is your willingness to apply your abilities. Simply stated, you are going to have to practice what you preach. Now that you have made that agreement with yourself to swim proficiently, apply it. Set your goals. Decide on your current level of conditioning and skills. Chart a course and write it down. Test your progress. Adjust your training plan, if necessary.

Technique is critical to swimming successfully. Since the freestyle stroke is the fastest stroke known, it is the only one you need to learn (backup strokes should include the breaststroke and backstroke). There are several special stroke techniques that triathletes employ, but these can be assessed after you have decided on a conditioning and skill-training program.

Your next step should be to go out and purchase some tools of the swimming trade: a comfortable suit (not a two-piece, but a one-piece of nylon or lycra); a plain latex cap; and goggles that don't leak. That's your total investment. (See Chapter 13, Tools of the Triathlon Trade, for more information.)

Breathing and Stroke Mechanics

Good breathing technique helps. Most pools are 25 yards in length, a distance that takes most lap swimmers at least seven to 10 breaths to complete. Completely exhale with your face in the water before rolling your head to one side to breathe. Breathe deeply. Many new swimmers fail to exhale completely and take only shallow, short breaths. You need all the oxygen that you can possibly inhale. Roll your head to the side; don't lift it up out of the water.

To acquire basic skills in stroke mechanics, take a class at your local community college, at the YMCA-YWCA, or at the Red Cross.

Controlling Your Pace: Heart-Monitored Training

Before you begin your training program you must calculate your target heart rate. You will try to stay at this rate during aerobic training.

Take your pulse by placing your fingertips against the carotid artery next to your throat (on the side of your neck) and count the number of heartbeats in one minute. Next, to estimate your maximum heart rate, subtract your age from 220. For example, if you're 40 years old, your maximum heart rate is 180 (220 - 40 = 180.) Take 80 percent of that figure to get your working-aerobic or target heart rate. If your maximum heart rate is 180, your target heart rate is 144 (180 x .80 = 144). If you keep your heart rate in the 130–140 range, you'll be benefiting aerobically from the workout.

Apply this calculation by taking your pulse at the end of the pool after swimming a couple of laps at a normal pace. Count your pulse for six seconds and multiply by 10 (simply add a zero). This gives you your rate for one minute. If it's above your computed working heart rate, you'll know that you're working too hard. If it is below that level, you are not stressing your cardiovascular system sufficiently.

With experience you will learn to control your pace to produce the target heart rate with ease. You will be breathing hard, but you won't be breathless. When this feeling becomes familiar, you can use it as a guide in pacing your swimming speed rather than stopping to take your pulse every time.

The table that follows contains a progressive 12-week program, with swimming sessions scheduled three times a week. If you swim more than three times a week or are already a pretty good swimmer, you may advance more quickly. Notice that the distance covered during the weeks slowly increases in simple progression from 1/4 mile to 3/8 mile to 1/2 mile to 3/4 mile and, on the last day, to

Table 4: Training Up to a One-Mile Swim
(72 laps in a 25-yard pool)
in Three Months

Week	Miles	Yards	Lengths	Swim Program (rest after each set)
1	1/4			18 × 1 length
2				9 × 2 lengths
3				6 × 3 lengths
4				1 × 18 lengths (non-stop)
5	3/8	675	27	1 × 18 plus
				1 × 9 plus
6				1 × 18 plus 9 × 2 (speed)
7	1/2	900	36	1 × 18 plus 3 × 6
8				2 × 18
9				1 × 27 plus 3 × 9
10	3/4	1,350	54	2 × 27
11				1 × 18 plus 1 × 36
12	1	1,800	72	1 × 72

Workout Frequency: Minimum of 3 nonconsecutive days per week
Maximum of 6 days per week

that great 1 mile continuous swim!

Time your first mile-long swim. This will be a landmark moment—one that you will want to use for time comparisons. Then continue your swimming program and, in several weeks, time yourself again. Record this information in your logbook so that you can progress. Set new goals, such as entering a Masters' swim meet, the swim leg on a triathlon relay, or a distance postal event, such as the Super Swim. Better yet, join a Masters swim club and enjoy the camaraderie and positive reinforcement of swimming with others.

CYCLING GOAL: 25 MILES CONTINUOUSLY

Cycling is unique among triathlon events in that it does not take weeks for the previously sedentary person to become involved in regular workouts. Even the most out-of-shape individual can start an exercise plan immediately after buying a good bike. If you are over the age of 35 and relatively sedentary, see your physician for a "go" sign to begin any type of aerobic workout.

In order to improve your cycling endurance capacity, you must know your current physical limits, then slowly and progressively work to push these limits higher. If you push too fast and hard, the "overuse syndrome" will impede your progress. If you push too slowly you will see little or no improvement. To achieve a balance you will have to listen to your body, which means to tune into your inner vital signs such as your heart rate, pulmonary rate, and muscle pains. This is a skill that you will learn only by riding your bike, not by reading the pages of this book.

There are basically two ways to approach an individualized cycling program: either measure miles or measure time in the saddle. Using the former approach, you progressively increase the number of miles and the frequency of cycling outings until you can ride continuously for 25 miles with no trouble. I prefer the latter: measuring time.

Begin with a 1/2 hour ride every other day at a steady pace at whatever intensity you can maintain and remain at the aerobic level during the ride. This will require pulse monitoring at first, until you learn the tempo required to keep your heart rate within the aerobic target range. If you live in an area with varied terrain, you should practice going up hills and work out on flat surfaces, to utilize the different muscle groups that different terrains require. In one or two workouts a week you should push yourself just a little above the normal cadence in the same gears for a specified period of time, mixing this with short breathers of slower pedaling. This faster pace will, in turn, become your normal pace in just a few months. This is the definition of the *training effect*.

You will notice that, as you push yourself to a pace you never thought you could keep up, very soon this pace seems easy. Push yourself just a little bit, because the chances are that you need to attain a better spin pace for your everyday cycling. But always

Rick Delantey takes off!

remember to "warm down" from bursts of speed by cycling slowly to release the buildup of lactic acid, which is the agent that can cause tight, cramped, or burning muscles.

The balance of your cycling training program should be designed around long, slow rides. For some of you, this may mean months of building from just a few minutes or miles. For others, this building may take place in just a matter of days. The following suggestions are guidelines for designing your own program—one that fits into your life's demands.

Beginning Training Schedule for Cycling

First two weeks—Cycle every other day for a distance of from four to ten miles. This will help you to break in new muscles that are used for spinning. Here is a sample workout schedule for the first two weeks:

- Monday: Ride four miles at a steady pace for about 24 minutes, keeping the heart rate at 65 percent of maximum.
- Tuesday: Rest
- Wednesday: Ride five miles at the same, six-minute-mile pace.
- Thursday: Rest.
- Friday: Repeat Monday's workout.
- Saturday: Do a longer ride, from 8–10 miles, but at a slightly slower pace, finishing in less than 70 minutes. Pick up the pace on the second Saturday, however.
- Sunday: Rest.

Weeks 3 and 4—Once you've broken in your "spinning" muscles, you should begin to relax and feel comfortable on the bike. Begin to cycle five times a week and from 5–15 miles at a time. For example:

- Monday: Ride at a faster pace for five miles in 25 minutes. This should not seem like too fast a pace, considering that marathon runners can cover 26 miles at this pace on foot.
- Tuesday: Rest.

- Wednesday: Try cycling six miles in 36 minutes, a slightly slower pace than Monday's.
- Thursday: Rest.
- Friday: Ride eight miles in 48 minutes.
- Saturday: This is your long workout day, so increase the distance to 15 miles in 90 minutes.

Weeks 5 and 6—Now begin to pick up the cadence and intensity of each workout. You should still cycle for five days, cycling for 5–20 miles per day. For example:

- Monday: Ride 7 miles in about 35 minutes, a five-minute-mile pace. This will start to boost your mileage and speed.
- Tuesday: Rest.
- Wednesday: Slowing the pace, cycle eight miles in 48 minutes and enjoy the workout and sights.
- Thursday: Rest.
- Friday: Repeat Monday's workout.
- Saturday: Finish the week with a 20-mile ride at a six-minute-mile pace, or ride continuously for 90 minutes, whichever you prefer.

Weeks 7 and 8—Your target is 25 miles continuously, and these are the days when you should be nearing that goal. Ride 5–25 miles, cycling six times per week. Example:

- Monday: Ride eight miles in about 40 minutes, which requires you to maintain a five-minute-mile pace.
- Tuesday: Rest as you ride on rolling hills or cycle an easy five miles in 35 minutes.
- Wednesday: Ride 10 miles in 60 minutes.
- Thursday: Rest.
- Friday: Repeat Monday's workout.
- Saturday: This is when you go for it! Try 25 miles at a pace you feel comfortable with, somewhere near a six-minute mile pace, finishing in two-and-a-half hours.
- As always, Sunday can be a rest day.

This schedule may be too difficult. If so, cut back. If it is too easy, add some anaerobic workouts. Pay attention to your body's signals. Record all the information in your training log. Maintain this schedule until it seems comfortable and then set a new goal—a new distance and time—and shoot for that. As you progress you will be adding a mix of hard interval workouts with long-distance rides of varying duration and pace. When you move out of the intermediate stage and into the highly competitive stage you will be using various types of training programs: sprint training, acceleration sprints, set sprints, slow and fast intervals, speed play, repetition riding, continuous slow riding, continuous fast riding.

Remember that you should warm up before beginning a ride. Warming up gradually raises your body temperature and increases your circulation, preparing your system for the work ahead, rather than jarring it into action. Some cyclists recommend stretching exercises; others recommend that you simply start slowly for the first five to 15 minutes until you feel comfortable and then begin your faster cadence.

A few quick tips to help make bicycling more enjoyable:

- Always carry a spare tube and pump in the event of a flat.
- Watch out for cars and dogs.
- Wear a helmet.
- Beware of boredom in your training program. Riding the same route day after day is bound to become boring sooner or later. Explore new routes and places. If you are self-conscious about your appearance, try riding in cycling shorts and shirt with the word *Campagnolo* across the chest; the public will think that you are an Italian racer!
- On the longer rides (over a half hour) you should take a water bottle.
- Try to do your rides before 9:00 A.M. or after 6:00 P.M.—it's cooler, the traffic is lighter, and there's less pollution. Also, most winds kick up during the middle of the day but are quiet in the morning and evening.

If you follow these simple guidelines, you will find that the minimum proficiency level of 25 continuous miles is easy to attain and can be done injury-free and with a ton of enjoyment. Pretty soon, cycling will become more than a fitness need for triathlon competitions; it will become an enjoyable part of your day-to-day life.

RUNNING GOAL: 5 MILES CONTINUOUSLY

For new athletes who have chosen running as a first sport, running five miles continuously will be the first of many important accomplishments. Five miles may seem a long distance at first, but it can be achieved relatively easily with a little determination. It then serves as an indicator of your having achieved a worthy level of fitness.

Running started the fitness revolution some 15 years ago, and Dr. Ken Cooper, with his book, *Aerobics* (New York, M. Evans & Co., Inc., 1968), was at the forefront. Even today it's still hard to find a better book to begin with for a good program and some fundamental information to serve as a firm foundation in aerobic fitness. Cooper did what no one else had done before him—he quantified this information, telling how many times a week and for how long you had to work out to get fit and what kinds of exercises qualified as aerobic. He told Americans how much, how long, and how hard they had to exercise—and he gave them a point system to measure their progress.

Of course, Cooper recommends a medical checkup before you start to run, especially if you're over 35. Realize that during the first few weeks of this program you'll be doing some walking— perhaps quite a bit of it. It's important that you not look at walking as a kind of defeat. Regard it, rather, as rest and recuperation for your system in between stints of running.

As with cycling, I recommend running by time rather than distance. Start with 15 minutes a day until this becomes a habit. Find a nice place to run-walk and do it with a friend if you can, but *do it*! Here is the procedure: Run as far as you can at a comfortable pace (you should be able to carry on a conversation) until you're out of breath. Then walk until you catch your breath. Then run again until you've been at it for 7 1/2 minutes, turn around,

Kathleen McCartney winning again.

and return (if you're on an out-and-back course). Or do it for 15 minutes if you're on a loop. (Loops seem easier at first.) Take your pulse at first to make sure you're not overdoing it, though the "talk test" is a pretty good way to estimate pace.

There are several cautions concerning running. First, it's relatively hard on your muscles and joints, compared to swimming and cycling. A good pair of shoes can make a big difference here. But if you find yourself getting stiff and sore, take a day or two off, stretch gently, and be nice to your body.

Running is the most efficient and time-saving way to become aerobically fit; but you must take it slow and easy. Walk and run the 15-minute course four or five days a week until you can run all of it. Typically, that will be about 1 1/2–2 miles in distance. Just to be safe, run the same time (or distance) for two more weeks before you increase it. (If you get *really* impatient and feel *really* good, you can add five minutes *every other* run.) Then run for 20 minutes at every workout. If that's too much, your body will let you know. (See the information on the symptoms of overtraining in Chapter 9.) Hold this for two weeks. Again, add five minutes at every other workout for two weeks, then measure out a five-mile course and run it!

Running is difficult because most people think it ought to be easier. Compared to swimming and cycling, the skill level is lower, yet the intensity is higher. So people don't take it easy enough at first. They beat themselves up at it; they make running a macho trip. Avoid this temptation. Enjoy your beginning running, then find a fun run or a short race in which to try your skills out. Guess what? You'll discover that you come in far from last place and first in self-esteem.

Running need only take up 1/48 of your day (or 30 minutes) to be worthwhile. If you have had a difficult time staying with a running program, you need to look at the obstacles you have created:

"I don't have a place that is safe to run."
"I am too old to start now."

"I don't have the time; I am too busy."
"I don't have anyone to run with."
"I don't like the cold/hot weather."
"I don't like the boredom."

For each of these excuses there is a response that overcomes the objection. If you are boring, so will running be. Weather changes are part of life. The parks are full of joggers; go meet some. Buy a microwave oven and convert wasted cooking time into running time. You're never too old unless you're dead. There *is* a place that is safe to exercise, or grab a friend and run together.

I know that it works. It is in the application that people falter. Hitch your wagon to a star and then start running. For you see, you are the star in your own life. Try putting yourself first. Try taking responsibility for your life. You may find out that the rest of the world is doing exactly the same thing and succeeding!

8

pioneering your own program

The brook would lose its song if we removed the rocks.

People are always asking me what the best training program is for them. They seem to think that there is one formula that will work for triple fitness or one plan that will make us all inveterate and indefatigable athletes. My response to this complex question is to initiate a series of queries that begins the process of developing a program that works for each person—an individualized training program based on proper planning. The questions generally consider these factors:

- athletic background: the history of participation in aerobic sports
- personal experiences with injuries, or a tendency toward injuries.
- ambitions and goals
- time available for training and racing
- financial commitment to purchase the necessary triathlon equipment
- physical skills and athletic talent
- type of competition to be encountered
- past athletic success or lack of success

Listing these factors allows you to form a profile of yourself. That

The triple fit body of a trained triathlete.

picture, in turn, usually indicates how much time will be necessary to develop a program, how much intensity you can handle, where and how to begin—in total, it will give you a starting point. And since you must be responsible for your own existence, making your own decisions and living with them, only you can devise an appropriate plan for yourself.

When pioneering your own program you might find that a format like the one below will work well for you. It is based on a four-stage progression that builds on the strength, speed, endurance, skill, and confidence that you develop as you travel toward whole-body aerobics. The program is based on six decisions that you must make:

1. Training feature: what the purpose of the training is to be
2. Training period: how long you estimate you will need to complete this set of workouts
3. Daily training ranges: the distances to be handled on a daily basis
4. Training frequency: how many workouts per day
5. Training mileage per week: how many miles and yards will be covered during the training week
6. Training benefits: the outcome of the training program (probably the most important decision)

FOUR-STAGE TRAINING MODELS AND METHODS

Stage 1: Build base and skills
Stage 2: Build a bigger base and better skills
Stage 3: Sharpen
Stage 4: Peak

The sound approach is to build general endurance first and to improve specific skills over a long period of time. Among other things, this reduces the risk of injury and keeps interest high. If you are just learning to bicycle or swim, for example, you will enjoy your training more if it is not painful and if you succeed. Keeping the pace down increases the likelihood that this will happen. Later

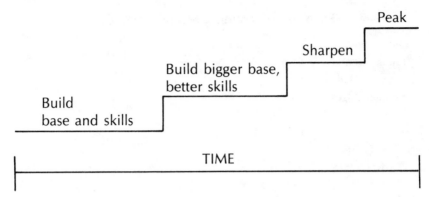

Four-Stage Crosstraining Program.

you can develop power and sharpness through a shorter period of intense training.

The crosstraining program charts this endurance-building/ strength-peaking progression in four stages. The length of time that you spend on each stage depends on you—your history, skills, initial fitness level, circumstances, and determination. As the creator of your own fitness, you might find that you prefer a five- or 10-stage plan. Great! Design one! It probably will work better for you. The length of time that you spend at each level can be determined only by listening to your body and how it is adapting itself to the training stage you are at. Through self-administered time trials, you will note progress. When that progress meets your goals and requirements, climb a step to the next level.

As you progress, *listen to your body*! You will be placing new demands on it. It will respond by becoming more fit, but it will also experience aches and pains. Note these in your training log; injury may not be far away.

TRAINING MODEL, STAGE #1: BUILD BASE AND SKILLS

To help you develop your own program I have composed a hypothetical training model, complete with specific objectives. As we progress through this model I will explain some of the complications and changes.

Example of Training Model Stage #1

Training feature:	Build base and skills
Training period:	Four weeks to one year
Daily	
Training ranges:	Swim: 500–2,000 yards
	Bicycle: 5–25 miles
	Run: 2–10 miles
Training frequency:	Six to seven workouts per week, one per day
	Swim—2 times per week
	Bicycle—2 times per week
	Run—2 times per week
	Weakest—1 additional time per week

Training benefits:

Goals: To follow this program consistently without missing a day (unless ill/injured)

To incorporate the triathlon training program into my lifestyle

Good Habits: To practice eating only what is needed to feed my muscles, not my fat

To practice the discipline to train daily

To practice the proper techniques of each sport

Sacrifice: To sacrifice my favorite sport to the benefit of all three

To sacrifice the money for proper equipment

To sacrifice the time required to practice good habits

Overload: To attempt on a weekly basis to stress beyond my normal limits in at least one sport.

Specificity: To cycle to train for bicycling

To stroke to train for swimming

To run to train for running

Adaptation: To watch for changes indicating training stress

To note those adaptations in my log book

Intensity: To train following the specific Stage 1 sequence of hard and easy, without variation

Preparation: To learn time planning

To keep a triathlon training log

Self-Testing: To begin the max mets self-testing program

Variety-Play: To enjoy the training experience

The purpose of the first stage is to build an aerobic endurance base and to begin skill development. Time to don the Speedo, pump up the tires, and lace up the running shoes. At first, you will seem rusty in everything except your primary sport, and the other sports may be entirely new to you. Start out easy on yourself and progress gently. If you find that the workouts you devise are too difficult, *change them.* Allow yourself to develop confidence. As the weeks pass, workouts will become easier and more enjoyable, the equipment and the terrain more familiar.

As you plan each stage of your program, make contracts with yourself. A contract is an agreement stating that you will train to meet certain standards. If you complete the contract, reward yourself—there are plenty of toys in the triathlon playground to give yourself. Develop a sense of continuity, a regular routine with a specific time to train set aside. Make an agreement with yourself to train on a uniform schedule, planning your days at least one day in advance. That way, training becomes automatic. Researchers have found that those who train in the early morning are the most persistent. At dawn, pollution is at a minimum, traffic is low, and the day's first light is inspiring.

During the building stage the crosstraining process should truly become part of a health and fitness lifestyle and should include good habits such as sleeping regular hours and eating foods that fuel your muscles, not your fat. Also, shop around for your equipment. Do some research. Spend a little time and learn what features you need in running shoes and how a 10-speed works. Then you can make informed choices. Having the right gear increases comfort and your level of interest.

Time planning begins as you try to squeeze three sports into your already demanding day. A training log will be your monitor—if you are not spending enough time, it will show that the contract is in jeopardy. It is difficult to develop this training habit, but that is common. You won't always be able to follow the schedule exactly; the rest of life just interrupts. Don't worry—habits grow with time. Eventually you will learn to enjoy the experiences on a daily basis. In preparing for my first Hawaii International Triathlon I discovered

Text continues on page 100.

Training Schedule, Stage 1
Model Program

Distance: 2,000-Meter Swim/25-Mile Bicycle/14-Mile Run per Week
Frequency: Workouts—2 Swims/2 Bicycles/3 Runs
Feature: Build Base/Build Skills

Note: WU = Warm-up   CD = Cool-down   Distances without units are in yards

Day	Sport	Distance	Intensity	Feature	Benefit	Activity
Sun	Run	6 miles	hard	speed train	build leg speed	WU 5-min. walk. 5 mile fun run/race for time. CD 5-min. walk. Extra: Calisthenics
Mon	Swim	500 meters	easy	stroke mechanics	improve technique	WU 1 × 50 easy relaxed. Kick: 2 × 25 hard with board Pull: 4 × 50 easy, work on technique with pull buoy. Free: 6 × 25 out hard/back easy. CD 1 × 50 relaxed.
Tue	Run	6 miles	hard	hill train	build increased leg strength	WU 5-min. walk. Run: repeat hills at least 180 seconds. Rest between repeats 1-3 min. CD 2-min. walk/jog.

	or Self-Test Day	1½-mi. run 400-yard swim 3 mile bicycle		Time trial Max Mets	measure improvement	See Chapter 7. Note results in log
Wed	Bicycle	5 miles	easy	spin	build leg speed	WU Start slow and become comfortable. 4 miles, gear 65-75 inches on level ground, learn to shift to keep cadence constant at 60-90 rpm. Do some intervals at stoplights. CD Ride easy, slow down the spin.
Thu	Swim	1,500 meters	hard	overload	build endurance	WU 1 × 50 easy, stroke mechanics Kick: 4 × 50, rest 15 sec. Pull: 4 × 100, rest 30 sec. Free: Pyramid—continuous swim—1 length slow, 1 length fast, 2 lengths slow, 2 lengths fast, 4 lengths slow, 4 lengths fast, 3 lengths slow, 3 lengths fast, 1 length slow, 1 length fast. CD 1 × 50 slow and easy.
Fri	Run	3 miles	easy	variety	relax/fun	An easy 3-mile jog with a friend.

Continued

Training Schedule, Stage 1
Continued

WU = Warm-up   CD = Cool-down   Distances without units are in yards

Day	Sport	Distance	Intensity	Feature	Benefit	Activity
Sat	Bicycle	20 miles	hard	overload	build leg speed and endurance	WU Ride easy, slowly increasing leg speed. Ride: vary the ride to include what you hate the most—hills, spinning, long rides and start to enjoy these. Try to relax and develop positive attitude.
Tue	Run	5 miles	hard	hill train	build increased leg strength	WU 5-min. walk. Run: repeat hills at least 180 seconds. Rest between repeats 1–3 min. CD 2-min. walk/jog.
or Self-Test Day		1½- mile run 400-yard swim 3-mile bicycle		time trial max mets	measure improvement	See Chapter 9. Note results in log.

Day	Activity	Distance				Description
Wed	Bicycle	5 miles	easy	spin	build leg speed	WU Start slow and become comfortable. 4 miles, gear 65–75 inches on level ground, learn to shift to keep cadence constant at 60-90 rpm. Do some intervals at stoplights. CD Ride easy, slow down the spin.
Thu	Swim	1,500 meters	hard	overload	build endurance	WU 1 × 50 easy, stroke mechanics. Kick: 4 × 50, rest 15 sec. Pull: 4 × 100, rest 30 sec. Free: pyramid—continuous swim—1 length slow, 1 length fast, 2 lengths slow, 2 lengths fast, 4 lengths slow, 4 lengths fast, 3 lengths slow, 3 lengths fast, 1 length slow, 1 length fast. CD 1 × 50 slow and easy.
Fri	Run	3 miles	easy	variety	relax/fun	An easy 3-mile jog with a friend.
Sat	Bicycle	20 miles	hard	overload	build leg speed and endurance	WU Ride easy, slowly increasing leg speed. Ride: vary the ride to include what you hate the most—hills, spinning, long rides—and start to enjoy these. Try to relax and develop positive attitude.

that I dreaded swim workouts. It was winter, and I despised the cold. Yet, as I progressed, I learned to look forward to my morning at the pool. Why? Probably because, as my skills sharpened, workouts became easier, the motion more fluid, the environment more familiar.

Stage 1 should last a minimum of four weeks; for some it should last at least a year. You should be able to reach your training ranges on a regular basis. The training frequency is one workout per day, and you may want to schedule a complete rest day. If this helps, do so. The specifications in the model I have drawn up probably represent the bare minimum necessary for a firm triathlon foundation.

When it is time to take the step to the next stage, you will know it. Your improvement in self-testing scores, the progressive ease of your workouts, and your ability to train easily through a week's schedule will indicate your readiness. As your body accepts the overloads that you have introduced, it responds by becoming fitter—developing the necessary strength, metabolic processes, and other adaptive changes. The result is that the same workouts become easier. The overload zone becomes the comfort zone. It now becomes necessary to increase the demands, to add overload, and to step up to the next tritraining stage.

TRAINING MODEL, STAGE #2:
BUILD A BIGGER BASE AND BETTER SKILLS

At Stage 2, you design the workouts so that they increase aerobic capacity and improve techniques. You now are adding a first story to the foundation. No longer should the media of water, roads, and trails seem uncomfortable. You should now consider yourself confident but not expert. You have developed the good habit of regular exercise and found that it is an important part of your day. You are a fledgling, novice, excited practitioner: you are now a "preppy" triathlete.

The training period for Stage 2 is four weeks to six months, again

Text continues on page 105.

Example of Training Model Stage #2

Training features: Begin triathlon sequence training to build bigger base and better skills.

Training period: 4 weeks to 6 months

Daily training ranges: Swim: 1,000–2,000 yards
Bicycle: 10–40 miles
Run: 5–12 miles

Training frequency: 9 workouts per week—5 days of single workouts; 2 days of double workouts
Swim—3 times per week
Bicycle—3 times per week
Run—3 times per week

Training mileage per week: Swim—4,500 meters
Bike—90 miles
Run—27 miles

Training benefits:

Goals: To learn the multiple-workout training program

Good Habits: To practice the skill of spinning
To practice the skill of running efficiently
To practice the skill of fluid freestyle stroke mechanics

Sacrifice: To sacrifice increased time for training

Overload: To initiate the long workouts in all three sports separately

Specificity: To begin weight training to build specific muscle groups used for each sport

Adaptation: To train past the soreness stage

Intensity: To learn pacing in all three sports

Preparation: To plan a system to help you improve in your weakest area

Self-Test: To improve on your max mets test scores

Variety-Play: To challenge yourself to new experiences
To enjoy your weakest sport

Training Schedule, Stage 2

Model Program

Distance: 4,500-Meter Swim/90-Mile Bicycle/27-Mile Run per Week
Frequency: 2 doubles and 5 single days for 9 workouts
Feature: Build bigger base, better skills

Note: WU = Warm-up   CD = Cool-down   Distances without units are in yards

Day	Sport	Distance	Intensity	Feature	Benefit	Activity
Sun	Bicycle	40 miles	hard	continuous slow riding	aerobic cycling	At slower-than-race pace: Cycle continuous 10 miles in same gear. Rest stop at least 10 min. Eat something. Ride 10 more continuous miles; continue this for 40 miles.
	Run	7 miles	hard	sequence training	back-to-back training experience	Run: Immediately dismount. Put on your running shoes and run at 90% of race pace for 7 miles. Drink fluids.
Mon	Swim	1,000 meters	easy	stroke	improve	WU 1 × 100 swim, loosen up. Kick: 4 × 50 with 15 sec. rest with board. Free: crawl 10 × 25 on 30 seconds. Kick: 2 × 100 with board. CD 1 × 250, relaxed.

Day	Activity	Amount	Intensity	Type	Goal	Description
	Weights	light	easy	learn how	increase strength	Spend 15–20 minutes.
Tue	Bicycle or Self-Test Day	30 miles	hard	Continuous *Fast Riding*	leg speed shifting skills	WU Begin slow and increase spin for 5 miles. CFR: 4 × 5 miles with 5 min. rest, faster than race pace. CD Easy 5 miles, decreasing heart rate slowly.
	See Training Schedule, Stage 1 **Tue**					
Wed	Run	12 miles	hard	pacing	learn racing speed	WU Easy 1-mile walk/jog. Pace Training: select a pace 15–60 sec. slower per mile than race pace. Run at that pace for 8 miles. CD easy 1-mile cool-down jog.
	Weights	medium			become comfortable, increase strength	Spend 15–20 min.
Thu	Swim	1,500 meters	easy	stroke	improve arm pull	WU 1 × 200, easy. Pull: 4 × 100 with 30 seconds. Free: 2 × 200 stroke mechanics work. Pull: 8 × 50 with 10 sec. recovery. CD 1 × 100 loose.

Continued

103

Training Schedule, Stage 2
Continued

Day	Sport	Distance	Intensity	Feature	Benefit	Activity
Fri	Run	8 miles	easy	play	enjoyment	Your choice as long as it is LSD (long, slow distance) and you have fun.
	Weights	light	easy	increase	strength	Workout should be more familiar/easier.
Sat	Swim	2,000 meters	hard	LSD	aerobic swimming condition	Free: 1 × 1,000 continuous, 5 min. rest. 1 × 1,000 continuous, time each try for negative split.
	Bicycle	20 miles	hard	POT = *Plenty of Tempo*	aerobic bicycle condition	WU 5 miles easy, next alternate, 1 mile POT (*Plenty of Tempo*) in lowest gear, followed by 1 mile easy for 10 miles; CD 5 miles easy.

[1]LSD refers to long slow distance, a phrase coined by Joe Henderson to refer to "natural running," or running at a pace and speed that is comfortable (flowing).

[2]Negative split refers to the way in which a workout is divided into two parts with the last part being faster in pace than the first part.

[3]Plenty of tempo is another way of saying a zesty pace or spin.

depending on your athletic promise and your training dedication. At this point you will increase the ranges of your workouts and begin the double workout—two sports per day. This program should require about nine workouts per week: five days of singles and (probably) two days of doubles. The doubles would be best scheduled back to back and in race sequence. During this stage you are going to practice pacing, do the long workout, and possibly engage in some weight training. You will discover new muscle soreness, improve in your weakest sport, and encounter new experiences.

You are going to note some changes in yourself; write them down in your log. For example, I have found that my need for sleep increases during this stage: I rise and set with the sun, a solar athlete. Pay attention to possible personality changes. If you become grouchy or irritable, realize that these are signals that something, such as overtraining, could be affecting you.

You might need to change your diet. Since the energy demands of the sports are increased, you might alter your selection of foods. Step on the bathroom scale, measure your "dry" weight, and record the information. Take a cloth tape and make a few girth measurements, such as chest, upper arm, thighs, and calves. Record this anthropometric data. Check your pulse when you first awake, before rising from bed. This is your true resting pulse. Watch for a rise in the resting pulse. A rise of 10 beats per minute could indicate that you're overloading your body and not giving it enough time to recover from the stress of training.

As you travel through the tritraining stages, always remember to start each workout with a warmup (WU) and conclude it with a cool-down (CD). Your body can be injured by immediate exposure to intense demands. It is best to allow the cardiovascular system to come up to operating temperature slowly, gently flexing the joints and gradually exerting the muscles. Develop a warm-up routine that suits your idiosyncrasies and preferences. Some athletes prefer static stretching to maintain flexibility. Others—myself included—apply the specificity principle to both warm-up and cool-down. In other words, you warm up and cool down by doing the activity that you've scheduled as a workout. If you're going for a ride, for example, warm up and cool down on the bicycle, on a flat terrain, at a relaxed pace. Several minutes of cool-down are as important as that time you spend warming up.

Pulse monitoring is extremely important for those who need help with judging exercise intensity. Learn to take the six-second pulse test to determine your target heart rate, as discussed earlier.

Stage 2 is designed to tune your technique. This is one of the cornerstones for your future growth. Learn to execute properly the kinesthetic requirements of each activity. Practice proper stroke mechanics, concentrate on running form, and develop your bicycling technique.

You may be fit enough to begin your crosstraining program with Stage 2. Fine. If you already have an endurance base and skills, there is no need to include Stage 1 training. Others can even begin with Stage 3. The point is to write your program so that it fits your current level of conditioning as well as fitting into the amount of time you can make available. During this stage you will view yourself in a new light. In dealing with a commitment to three different sports, you will relate to new friends and learn the language and systems of new endeavors. It will probably be one of your most enjoyable stages because it includes the dynamics of exploring new terrain and experiences. Good luck and smooth riding, running, and stroking.

TRAINING MODEL, STAGE #3: SHARPEN

Increases in intensity need to be written into the program as you throw the power switch toward increases in both duration and speed. At this stage you begin the triple workout, or minitriathlon, on a weekly basis. You will still incorporate days of overdistance, but you'll begin to add speed training to supplement those long workouts.

Text continues on page 111.

Example of Training Model, Stage #3

Training features: Sharpen all skills, all cardiovascular components;
mental toughness

Daily
training period: Four weeks to four months

Training ranges: Swim: 1,500–3,000 meters
Bicycle: 10–75 miles
Run: 5–15 miles

Training period:
Daily training
ranges: 12 workouts per week—3 days of single workouts; 3
days of double workouts; 1 day of a triple workout
Swim—4 times per week
Bicycle—4 times per week
Run—4 times per week

Training mileage
per week: Swim—7,000 meters
Bicycle—150 miles
Run—40 miles

Training benefits:

Goals: To learn the triple workout

Good Habits: To develop mental determination
To practice quality workouts

Sacrifice: To increase the intensity to improve performance

Overload: To combine the long workouts

Specificity: To train in the specific sequence of the triathlon race

Adaptation: To note the reaction to triple workouts

Intensity: To learn to rest on a training day
To learn to increase the number of hard days

Preparation: To plan the mental discipline required

Self-Testing: To continue to see max met improvement

Variety-Play: To throw fun days into the schedule

Training Schedule, Stage 3

Model Program

Distance: 7,000-Meter Swim/150-Mile Bicycle/40-Mile Run per Week
Frequency: Swim 4 times, bicycle 4 times, run 4 times—12 workouts
Feature: Sharpen skills and fitness

Note: WU = Warm-up   CD = Cool-down   Distances without units are in yards

Day	Sport	Distance	Intensity	Feature	Benefit	Activity
Sun	Swim	1,000 meters	hard			1 × 1000.
	Bicycle	25 miles	hard	triathlon workout	specific training	1 × 25 miles.
	Run	5 miles	hard			1 × 5 miles.
Mon	Run	10 miles	easy	play day	relax and rest while training	Any pace, as long as it is easy, enjoyable, relaxing.
	Weights					
Tue	Swim	1,500 meters	hard	intervals	strength	WU 1 × 100 loosen up. Pull: 10 × 50 on 60 seconds. Kick: 5 × 50 on 1½ minutes. Free: 6 × 100, fast. Swim Down: 1 × 50, easy.

Day	Activity	Distance	Intensity	Type	Purpose	Description
	Bicycle or Self-Test Day (See Stage 1)	40 miles	hard	hills	increase leg strength	WU 2 miles, easy. Ride: 36 miles of continuous hills. CD 2 miles, easy.
Wed	Swim	3,000	easy	continuous slow swim	overdistance training	Two Options: a) 1 × 1,500 with 5 min. rest. 1 × 1,500 stop. b) 1 × 3,000, time yourself.
	Weights					
Thu	Bicycle	10 miles	hard	CFR (Continuous Fast Riding)	leg speed aerobic	WU easy 1-mile ride. Ride: nonstop 9 fast miles.
	Run	10 miles	hard	Fartlek	speed strength	WU 1-mile walk/jog. Fartlek: ½ mile faster than race pace, then 1 mile slower than race; alternate for 9 miles.

Continued

Training Schedule, Stage 3
Continued

Day	Sport	Distance	Intensity	Feature	Benefit	Activity
Fri	Run	15 miles	easy	long, slow distance	aerobic running	Continuous running at easy pace. Stop and drink water or eat.
	Weights					
Sat	Swim	1,500 meters	hard	stroke mechanics	improve technique	1 × 1,500, easy. Time.
	Bicycle	75 miles	hard	continuous slow riding	overdistance training	Rest every 25 miles for 5 minutes. Eat.

Consider the problems that might arise. A missed workout is difficult for many people to handle. The best solution to this problem is to go on to the next day; *do not* try to make up for the loss by adding those lost miles/meters/times to other days. Injury is one of the prices you might pay for making a sudden jump in your training load.

There is also the problem of inclement weather. Athletes who live in severe winter climates will find it difficult to train outdoors and adapt the program to meet these conditions. Take your training indoors with bicycle rollers, indoor tracks, and pools, where the temperature is more comfortable.

Where there is a will, there is a way. When there is not enough time in the day, if training is important enough, you will find time. No matter what the obstacle, you *can* design and write into your training program a way to exercise.

You may encounter a discipline problem in your weakest sport. The clues are lackluster or missed workouts because of other commitments. Counterattack with creativity. Invite a friend to participate, ride your bicycle to your favorite restaurant, swim in a different pool, or go to a fun run or race. Keep the days fresh with fun, and you will begin to enjoy your weak sport more and avoid it less.

The duration of Stage 3 is four weeks to four months. If you become eager to tackle that final stage, always remember that it is better to stay too long in a training stage than to jump ahead too soon. You will notice more changes as your body continues to adapt to the increased training. You will see muscle development and improvement in stamina. That's what a conditioning program is supposed to do—change your condition. Your outlook might be altered, too, as you see life through lenses focused on developing your body to its maximum aerobic fitness. Perhaps the only people you will want to see socially are other athletes. Maybe your non-athlete friends will find you an obsessive, judgmental bore.

Your progress here might not seem as noticeable as in the previous stages. You are now starting to fine-tune a smooth-running machine, and this may be the first time your body has been exposed to the stresses of crosstraining. It is your goal at this stage to direct your energy and attention to detail, to practice the triathlon specifically in order to improve on the triathlon.

The law of diminishing returns comes into play at this stage, meaning that improvement will require progressively more effort. As you approach the limits of human fitness, improvement in performance is not in direct proportion to the amount of training you invest; rather, you must put in an increasing amount of effort for smaller returns. Each percentage point of fitness and skill improvement costs more than the previous point. It is that last, hard-won 10 percent that makes the difference between a champion and an also-ran.

In Stage 3, you also concentrate on developing mental toughness. You are the source of your performance. You can't blame others, circumstances, or conditions. Some people may obstruct you and some may help enthusiastically, but you are the one who either puts them off or invites them aboard. You determine your own success and your own failure.

Discovery and experimentation characterize this stage. You will be sore after some of the intense workouts. This is to be expected. Try food supplements (vitamins and minerals), hot tubs, massage, Shiatsu, and hanging upside down. The physiology of muscle soreness is not well understood—invent some therapies of your own.

In Stage 3 training, you must realize that you are beginning the ultradistance triathlon workout schedule. The training ranges are long and aerobic; the training mileage is high and requires a great deal of time. If you are interested in sharpening for the marathon or sprint triathlon, then simply write shorter-distance, higher-intensity workouts.

As you journey through the Stage 3 program you should carry with you the confidence that you are now a capable swimmer, runner, and cyclist. You are not yet fully refined in all three sports in sequence, but that will come in the last stage. For variety—and to stay fresh mentally—do some bicycle workouts with the local bike club, try your feet at some road races on the weekends, enter an age group distance swim or an open-water competition. Test your triathlon training program in single-event competition and give your adrenal glands a workout, too. You are now a journeyman triathlete.

TRAINING MODEL, STAGE #4: PEAK

Congratulations on achieving triple fitness! It has been a tough and rigorous course, certifying you as a dedicated individual who loves to train in the pursuit of physical excellence. You have come a long way and should feel proud of your progress and your ability to stick with it.

You have written a new definition of yourself. You are no longer a single-fitness swimmer, runner, or cyclist. You are a triathlete, a triple-fitness individual. You have aptitudes, skills, and fitness levels that single-sport athletes have never known. I realized the value of these capabilities recently when I saw the fuel gauge of the car I was riding in register empty. I smiled, knowing that I could run miles to town, or bike from the most remote desert road, or swim across a lake to find a gas station. As a triathlete, your fitness prepares you for business, pleasure, or safety.

You are now a total athlete whose upper- *and* lower-body muscles have been developed aerobically. You should be pleased with the balance of muscle development. Triathletes have an advantage over all single-sport fitness freaks, for they have trained their bodies in ways that are ignored by specialized conditioning programs.

In designing your training program for the peak performance stage, you should aim for the following goals:

- Meet or exceed performance target times and paces;

- Perform all three sports in succession, possibly at full race distance in one day;

- Minimize mistakes (in equipment, pacing, eating, etc.), and correct mishaps (flat tire, stomachache, etc.).

This is a tough assignment, for if you are lax in one single component of the triathlon, all will suffer. The final tuning schedule requires that you crosstrain in both intensity and duration and that you accustom yourself to the same fuels and equipment you will use and the same conditions you will find on the day of the event. The results at this stage will separate the also-rans from the truly capable triathletes.

The Stage 4 training period should be short, as it is difficult to sustain such intensity for more than a month. Spend time instead on developing your race plan, which should include pacing, eating during competition, and contingency plans for mishaps.

During these final days most world-class athletes are training to their maximums. Certain problems tend to occur at this time.

Example

Training feature:	To peak mentally and physically
Training period:	1–4 weeks
Training ranges:	Swim: 1,500–5,000 meters
	Bicycle: 10–100 miles
	Run: 5 miles to a marathon
Training frequency:	13 workouts per week;
	3 single workouts per week
	2 double workouts per week
	2 triple workouts per week
	Swim—4 times per week
	Bicycle—4 times per week
	Run—5 times per week
Training mileage per week:	Swim—9,000 meters
	Bike—200 miles
	Run—50 miles

Training benefits:

Goals:	To be in prime shape in all three sports
Good Habits:	To practice using the same equipment that will be used during the race
	To practice eating the same foods that will be eaten during the race
	To practice in the same environment (heat/cold, hills/flat) that will be encountered during the race
Sacrifice:	To give the time required to complete the fine-tuning stages
Overload:	To vary and increase the combinations of the workouts in sequence
Specificity:	To train in the specific intensity of the triathlon
Adaptation:	To adapt to the effects of the intensity and the combinations of workouts
Intensity:	To accept the difficulty of the hard days
	To enjoy the workouts on the easy days
	To realize that the easy days now are what the hard days used to be
Preparation:	To develop the race plan strategy
Self-Testing:	To time-trial at half the distance of the triathlon events
Variety-Play:	To plan workouts in new environments/distances with different friends

Beware of injuries and watch out for stress-related viruses—colds, fever blister, stomach problems caused by a stressed immune system, etc. Illness is a signal from the body that you should reduce stress. I was reminded to heed this signal recently when I had a bout with bronchitis after completing a 100-mile footrace in just over 20 hours. I finally recognized that my body was asking for a vacation and did not want to be immersed immediately in my next sports challenge. I took four months off from serious training and returned refreshed (and eager and frustrated as well).

The Olympic imperative "Citius, Altium, Fortius" (swifter, higher,

Text continues on page 119.

Training Schedule, Stage 4

Model Program

Distance: 9,000-Meter Swim/200-Mile Bicycle/50-Mile Run per Week
Frequency: Swim 4 times, bicycle 4 times, run 5 times—13 workouts
Feature: Peak training

Note: WU = Warm-up   CD = Cool-down   Distances without units are in yards

Day	Sport	Distance	Intensity	Feature	Benefit	Activity
Sun	Swim	1,500 meters	hard			All three sports in succession at subrace pace, with minimal rest between, using same food, equipment, and support as on race day.
	Bicycle	35 miles	hard	sequence training	specific triathlon	
	Run	10 kilometers	hard		aerobic condition	
Mon	Run	13.1 miles	easy	over-distance	aerobic power	A continuous run with a friend over uneven terrain.

Day	Sport	Distance		Type	Purpose	Notes
Tue	Swim	1,000 meters	hard	intervals	speed	WU 1 × 50, loosen up. Pull: 5 × 50, fast. Kick: 4 × 25, fast. Free: 10 × 50 on 55 seconds. CD 1 × 50, easy.
	Bicycle	10 miles	hard	hills	leg strength	Pedal hard on the uphills and spin fast on the downhills.
	or Self-Test Day	at least ½ of race distance	hard	time trial for max mets	measure improvement	True time trial as if a race, but test only one sport per week.
Wed	Swim	2,000 meters	hard			Subrace pace, continuous.
	Bicycle	25 miles	hard			
	Run	8 miles	hard			

Continued

Training Schedule, Stage 4
Continued

Day	Sport	Distance	Intensity	Feature	Benefit	Activity
Fri	Swim	race distance	hard	time test	learn pace	The next two days are time trials. Try to do each event at the pace that you think you can maintain during the race. Clock it. Learn pacing.
Sat	Bicycle	race distance	hard	time test	learn pace	Same as Friday.
	Run	race distance	hard	time test	learn pace	

stronger) applies to your development. You are now in the best overall condition of your life. You have made new acquaintances, learned new sports, discovered new experiences, developed a new concept of yourself. This is the total aerobic spirit. You are entering the stadium at or near your full potential.

It hasn't been easy. It hasn't happened quickly. Rarely are the prizes that we seek in life acquired easily or rapidly. It hasn't been without sacrifice. Rarely are the accomplishments that we strive for obtained without giving. It hasn't been without direction, for you have modeled yourself in pursuit of goals and good habits. It hasn't been without knowledge; for with the help of scientific principles you can grow toward achieving your full potential. It hasn't been without enjoyment, as you have had a lot of fun along the way.

This program is not an end in itself. Your goal is to complete a competitive triathlon successfully, to be the winner that each of us desires to be. We can all be victors in the challenges we set for ourselves. Some people are superwinners, driving themselves to achieve more than anyone else. But, when the contest is over, life still goes on and the next day brings fresh opportunities.

the triathlon log

"Fitness is health, and health is a habit. One of the best means of staying on the track, in lane, or on the road is to habitually record information from your workouts."

You can best evaluate your progress over an extended period of time by recording it. A log is a diary of the day-to-day ritual of training. It is the history of your program. Part of keeping fit is keeping a log.

Skip Swannack-Gibbs, a friend and competitor of mine, was the first woman to crack the 24-hour mark at the Western States 100-Mile Endurance Run in 1979. I was the third. Discussing the contest, we agreed that much better times were possible. She said that in order to train for a faster pace, her first step would be to review the past four years of her training log. As a physical education teacher, she knows from her experience with fitness development that the log is one of the main ingredients in the recipe for successful conditioning.

Skip said she would like to read other athletes' training logs in hopes that they might show ways of mixing the ingredients that she has not tested. Mike Catlin, two-time men's winner of the same race, made such an offer to her, she said, with the understanding that his log would not be photocopied. For many athletes, training logs are private diaries that are not to be shown to others—certainly not to the competition. For Skip, they provide an opportunity to share training regimens, the highs and lows of workouts, the practical application of the fitness commandments. These are the kinds of benefits that triathletes can gain from one another when training logs are shared.

BASIC ENTRIES FOR YOUR TRAINING LOG

Training Rating System

Being curious about how others have maintained their logs, I queried friend and fellow athlete Steve Madison one night about his log. At first he darted a quick glance of suspicion in my direction. Then, remembering that we are training comrades, he walked over to the bookshelf. Neatly in order by year were six small mysterious-looking black books. Steve's training logs were relatively simple, small notebooks with the year printed in gold numbers on the spine.

His written remarks included how he felt about the workout, what he thought or discussed with friends, the types of pains or concerns he was feeling, comments on improvements from previous runs, notations on vitamins, the weather, observations about the terrain, even his bowel problems.

Always, the date, sport, distance, and time were followed by a number. Each number was a 3−, a 3, or a 3+. I asked for an explanation. He replied that this was his rating system, with a 5 meaning a zenith performance and a 1 an effort not worth lacing on his shoes for. Reviewing several years worth of data, I saw that there were no 5s or 1s in his records. Steve said that he is saving the 5 for the perfect day, and he has not yet experienced the worst of all possible training runs, a 1. Most of his training runs were rated as average: a 3. Some were slightly better, a 3+, and some were slightly worse, a 3−, but no euphoric 5s or miserable 1s appeared.

Regardless of the numerical scale you use, the basic method of rating the workout is useful for analyzing progress. Register the number that you feel describes each experience.

Pulse Rates

There should also be space in your log for two different pulse measurements for each workout. Most physiologists feel that the postexercise recovery rate is a key indicator of cardiovascular fitness. To gauge the recovery rate, take your heart rate immediately after stopping exercise and then again 90 seconds later. Note the difference between the two figures. As your cardiovascular fitness improves, the difference between the two figures will increase, thus indicating a faster recovery rate.

As discussed earlier, the best way to measure your heart rate is to use either a digital watch or one with a sweep second hand. Counting beats for longer than six seconds tends to lead to inaccuracies because your pulse rate drops rapidly at the cessation of exercise, especially when you are in good condition.

Upon awakening in the morning, before you rise from bed, take your resting pulse. Most likely you will notice great variations over time. My morning pulse rate usually varies between 58 and 64, depending on such factors as stress, alcohol consumption, sleep quality and duration, and altitude. Your resting pulse rate should be used as a control guide for your training program. If it is more rapid than usual, your body is signaling you to slow down. You are training too hard. If you notice that your pulse is elevated for several days, then your body is announcing a pending breakdown. It indicates that your immune system is fighting an intrusion, that your stress level is too high, that your training schedule is not allowing sufficient recuperation, or that you have some other systemic problem. Take heed of this early warning and modify your day's activities, perhaps even your training regimen.

Description

A daily commentary is very useful, even though its contents will be more descriptive than quantifiable. In this space, report your experience—the who, what, when, where, why, and how of the day. Spend the extra time and ink to comment about your health, happiness, and fitness; an animal encountered in the wild; or a conversation with a fellow athlete. This will be the part of the diary you will return to most frequently as you revive memories of rides, races, swims, and runs that you loved or loathed.

Summary

The triathlon training log that I use features space for a summary of the week's distance, the average distance per day, and cumulative distance for the entire year. There is room for commentary on the week as a whole, plus a record of your body weight. Every fourth week, there is a page on which to summarize the month and to comment about your training program, physical condition, mental attitude, and goals.

Charts are included for plotting week-by-week distances for each of the three sports during the course of a year. You might want to photocopy a page and put it up on your bulletin board at home or work (I prefer the refrigerator because I associate the energy input with exercise output). Watch your progress as you build a better base and better skills during the year. Record this on a Yearly Distance Summary, which offers you comparisons for distance by month in swim, bicycle, and run sports.

A Record of Races is the place to note your times and assess your progress as you enter different races during the year. These can be truly competitive events or your self-testing time trials. The log design is flexible, so adapt it for your own particular system.

Copies of my triathlon training log can be purchased for $5 (including postage and tax) from Fleet Press, 2410 J St., Sacramento, CA 95816.

TRAINING BALANCE: OVERTRAINING VS. UNDERTRAINING

The key to training is balance— to keep your discipline, demand, overload, speed, intensity, relaxation, and recuperation at such a

Sample Training Log Format

Day	Date		Sport	Distance	Time	Pulse	Commentary
S	14	AM	Run-Race	10K	42:10	72	Raced hard at Golden State Women's Run. Finished in 25th place - GREAT!!
		PM					Rested
M	15	AM	Swim	1,000yds	25	48	Easy work out - Crawl
		PM					
T	16	AM	Bicycle	20 mi	1.0		Rode hard on bike trail, legs felt easy/ warmed
		PM	Swim	2,500yds	1.5		Work out with Masters Swim at YMCA
W	17	AM	Run	5 mi	60 min		Ran repeat hills - ugh!!
		PM					
T	18	AM	Bicycle	25 mi	1.3		Met Kathy & did loop in the city
		PM	Swim	300yds			workout w/ Masters
F	19	AM					
		PM	Run	10 mi	90 min		Met group & ran easy - then out for pizza
S	20	AM	Bicycle	50 mi	4 hrs.		Group rides through foothills
		PM					Am enjoying the swimming more, the race time was excellent. It is all staying together.

	Swim	Bicycle	Run
Week's Total	4,500	95	21
Week's Average	928/13.4		3
Year—To Date	12,500	7,500	660

Weight 130   Week # 22

Four-Week Summary Format

	SWIM	BICYCLE	RUN
Four Week:			
Total Distance:	_____	_____	_____
Longest Workout:	_____	_____	_____
Year-to-Date Total:	_____	_____	_____

COMMENTS About Training Program:

_____

_____

_____

COMMENTS About Physical Condition:

_____

COMMENTS About Mental Attitude:

_____

COMMENTS About Goals:

_____

fine balance that you achieve maximum results with a minimum of downtime.

A training log will help guide you to this balanced condition. One of its primary functions is to monitor your body's responses and store the data for review. Ideally, and probably in the not too distant future we will have physiological monitoring equipment in the home that will spew out the same information scientists now use to write exercise prescriptions for their athletes: blood analysis that gives pH, lactate, and other levels; hair analysis that monitors levels of minerals, vitamins, substrates; treadmills, bicycle ergometers, or swimming tanks that analyze not only stroke mechanics but heart response, Max VO_2 (maximum oxygen uptake), and anaerobic thresholds.

Right now, for example, several computerized training programs for runners are currently available, as reported in the June 1982 issue of *Runner's World*. These programs don't offer detailed physiological monitoring, but they will store a limitless amount of data and give you just about any kind of training analysis you want. The discs aren't very expensive (about $40–50); but, of course, you will need a home computer such as a TRS-80, and the minimum cost you'll be able to get by with is about $200.

Computerized training programs are sophisticated means of analyzing and spotting trends in your training. You can program your body weight, calories consumed, resting pulse, minutes run, miles run, quality of effort, subjective feelings, and other variables. This data is then stored and can be graphed at the end of a specified period of time, say, a month. You can, for example, graph your morning pulse against the miles run the previous day or miles run against your subjective feelings at the end of the day.

Athletes interested can contact several sources about programs:

1. J. S. Clay, "PHYPRO," Softrum Specialties, 6 Purdue Lane, North Dartmouth, MA 02747.

2. American Sports Data, "Quality Mileage Computer," 31 Rockledge Road, Hartsdale, NY 10530.

3. John Graham, "RACE LOG '82," 109 Kelvington Drive, Monroeville, PA 15146

Without a computer, athletes can still maintain their balance through pulse monitoring and log books. The body will give you signals when you are either overtraining or undertraining. Remember that these conditions usually begin slowly and continue to get worse.

To diagnose overtraining, scientists love to measure the quality of ketosteroids in your urine or look at the increases in your white blood cells (eosinophils), distortions in the T-waves in electro-

Symptoms of Overtraining and Undertraining

Overtraining

Persistent feeling of general tiredness during training or during the remainder of your day.

Legs that feel like lead when you are walking or climbing stairs or legs that throb.

An abnormal increase in the amount of sleep required; restlessness, your mind spinning at 100 rpms; irritability; insomnia.

During your workout a) your heart rate does not drop below 120 beats per minute after five minutes' rest b) respiratory rate is higher than 12–16 breaths per minute.

Feeling emotionally upset, easily agitated, anxious after a workout.

Poor performances at workouts/races.

Joint and muscle pains with no apparent injury.

Hives, rashes, nausea, head colds, and stuffy nose.

Undertraining

Increase in body weight that does not appear, from a naked mirror analysis, to be caused by increased muscle mass or fat.

Making excuses not to train because you are too busy.

cardiographic tracings or, better still, increases in the activity of the enzymes creatine phosphokinase (CPK) and glutamic oxalic transaminase (SGOT). But alas, none of these are useful to you because of the time, equipment, and specialized training required to administer and interpret the tests accurately. This doesn't even include a consideration of the expense involved.

Instead, let's look at some of the signs that have proven to be the most reliable indicators of overtraining or undertraining (see page 127). Bear in mind that some of these symptoms indicate conditions other than undertraining and overtraining. Therefore, don't be rushed in your diagnosis. If, however, these symptoms persist, overtraining or undertraining is probably the culprit.

Preventing over/undertraining is always preferable to relieving the condition. If you have been overtraining, it is better to reduce the intensity of your workouts than the total mileage. If you have been undertraining, it's a good idea to reassess your goals and revise your training schedule. You will have lost fitness, and continuing on your previous schedule could lead to injury. It is recommended that you do low-intensity workouts for one to three days; if the symptoms do not disappear, allow two to five days for complete rest. Be aware that other stressors exist in life and that reducing them before they reach dangerous levels is of critical importance for prevention of the over/undertraining syndrome.

RACE PREPARATION

Remember the training days when everything was easy? It seemed that no one could keep up with your aerobic pace and that it was difficult to tire yourself even at your fastest cadence. If only such power could peak on race day!

It's possible. A training log will let you predict which day will get a perfect rating! Here's how: Study all of the preceding days in the month prior to a day that gets your highest rating. The formula will slowly come into perspective as you isolate variables and begin to link factors that lead to your peak performances in the training cycle.

MEMORIES

Training is the best part of my day. It is a time when I am free from the helter-skelter atmosphere of my professional workday. There are no telephones to disrupt my thoughts. There are no problems that can't wait until my return. It is a refreshing time. Experiences on the road or in the pool, people that I meet while working out, breakdowns, new shoes, new running routes offer both beauty and challenge. Recently, for the first time in my life, I ran on new snow in a Sierra sugar pine forest with a close friend. It was such a sensual experience to feel the snow, the softness of the pine needles underfoot, and the comfort of traveling stride for stride with a comrade.

Your log is the place to describe these experiences, to return to those wonderful moments. It makes for fine reading.

The training log is a record to which you can continually return and which you can examine for trends. You'll want to ask these questions:

"Why did I do well in this race and not in that one?"

"Why did I become injured?"

"Were there indications from my training that I was getting a bad cold?"

If you note that you are having a string of workouts that you rate less than average, the message is staleness, boredom, a need for change. If you note that the ratings are above average, then you are doing well, enjoying the experience, and probably becoming more fit.

Your ability to analyze the log over an extended period of time is critical. Go back frequently and look for trends, as they are the precursors of successes and failures. The triathlete's 10 commandments relate directly to the training log. In particular, remember Commandment #2: Thou shalt maintain continuity and discipline (principle: good habits). Practice the good habit of writing in your training log every day.

10

the fine-tuned triathlete

"If you train just your sport-specific muscles—those used in cycling, swimming, or running—it is like having a stereo sound system with a great amplifier and lousy speakers. If you trained your amplifier—your heart—through running but not your upper body through swimming, it would be like buying stereo speakers from a five-and-dime with an expensive stereo amplifier from the finest audio shop."

So you are in training for a triathlon. You can swim, cycle, and run. Your muscles are strong; your aerobic capacity is well developed. With enough conditioning at long distances in each event you know you can complete even the ultratriathons. Perhaps you want to be more than an also-ran. Maybe you dream of placing high, even winning. If you are already an experienced triathlete, your goal may be to better your time in each event. Conditioning and desire are simply not enough.

Again, athletic achievement stands on a sturdy tripod: (1) talent—what you are given to work with; (2) dedication—where you take your abilities; and (3) technique—how you perform physical tasks. You may have marvelous natural gifts and the spirit of a zealot, but if your technical execution is poor, your potential is being wasted.

Fine-tuning means adjusting your equipment and your skill to precision accuracy. You will need to correct bad habits and thus pour more of your hard-driving energy into relentless speed. No one ever won a medal for splashing the most water or pushing the most air or pounding the pavement the hardest. Sustained velocity is the only meaningful measure of race performance. Fine-tuning your technique will wrest several minutes from the clock because it adds the power and effects of knowledge to your strength and conditioning. Water, wind, and gravity: these are the media of the triathlete, and all offer resistance to motion. Added to these media is the body's inner resistance to constant, powerful exertion—the tendency of muscles, joints, and connective tissue to fatigue. Finally, there is fate's resistance to good fortune, those little stumbles and mistakes that make life an interesting but frustrating enterprise. Resistance is a diversion of power from primary purpose, a wastage that can be minimized through proper technique.

There are several fine-tuning techniques that you should attempt to add to your training regime. If you can follow these guidelines, you can save hours of wasted energy and damaged equipment.

SWIMMING

Arm and Upper-Body Motion

A proper crawl stroke carves a precise pattern both above and below the surface. The hand slips into the water edgewise with fingers together, the pinky side banking high and the palm outward at about 45 degrees. No flow-spoiling air bubbles are dragged under the water.

After entry the hand accelerates smoothly along a curved S-shaped course, directing all thrust rearward. Simultaneously the body rolls along its long axis about 35 degrees to allow the opposite arm its recovery above water. Crawl-stroke swimmers spend more time on their sides than they spend in a flat position. As the illustration shows, from the swimmer's rolling frame of reference, the hands sweep arcs toward the chest; but from a pool frame of reference, the hands are first pulling and then pushing

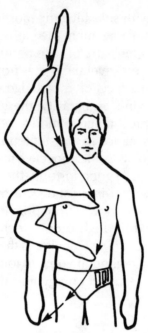

The arm pull and push pattern from the swimmer's reference for the freestyle stroke.

in a constant quest for dead still water. Nonmoving water presents the swimmer with resistance to push or sweep against, as opposed to moving water, which decreases the pull power of the stroke.

The Stroke

The leading arm flexes to a right-angle elbow bend as it pulls along from entry to just under the chest, then unflexes as it pushes through to the hip. Simultaneously the wrist is first angled inward sharply so that the palm faces rearward. Then, as the pull progresses, the wrist straightens until it is even with the forearm just as the push begins. Throughout the push phase the wrist flexes progressively backward, thus keeping the palm facing rearward, always at a pitch that deflects water backward. At the end of the thrust the wrist swivels so that the palm faces the hip, and the hand then slides out of the water as if it were slipping out of a hip pocket.

Above water, the arm reaches forward while staying close to the body's centerline. The hand speeds by the ear on its way to reentry, elbow flexed considerably. The swimmer's head is submerged to the forehead, face angled forward slightly except when it turns to the side for a breath in the wave trough just in front of the shoulder. Breath is inhaled when the arm opposite the breathing side reenters and is exhaled evenly in the water. As you can clearly see from the illustration below, the entire freestyle stroke is a specific set of movements.

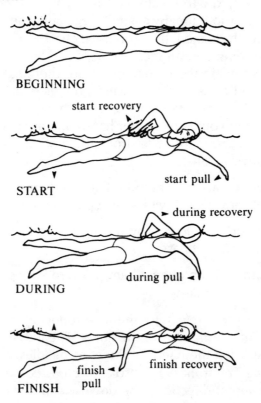

The entire freestyle stroke pattern.

The competitive freestyle stroke has changed considerably over the past 20 years. Today's stroke style emphasizes two major concepts that improve technique:

1. decreasing the resistance to forward motion;

2. increasing the propulsive forces of forward motion.

The success of champion swimmers is based on their ability to apply these concepts. So, how can you increase your propulsive force and move through the water faster?

You simply increase your *hydrodynamic lift* and decrease your *drag.* By shaping your hands like the wings of an airplane and moving them rapidly to create lift force, you can increase your hydrodynamic propulsion. By carefully regulating the pitch of your hands and feet throughout the propulsive phases, you can achieve a decrease in drag and an increase in lift.

Let's try to explain these concepts more thoroughly. Think of your hands and arms as if they were propellers on an airplane (which, in reality, are rotating wings). By changing direction and pitch throughout your stroke, your hands and arms serve as a set of propeller blades. In freestyle stroke the motion can be broken into the following parts:

- Upon entry into the water the hand and arm move forward and then downward with a sweeping motion.

- This motion is followed by an inward and upward sweep through the pull phase.

- Finally, there is an outward and upward sweep through the push and exit phases.

The term *sweep* refers to the lift-producing, propeller-like vertical and lateral motions of the limbs. The old terms *pull* and *push* suggest using the hands and feet as paddles, a more drag-resistive form. The front crawl stroke, then, is composed of four sweeps in different directions: the downsweep, the insweep, the outsweep, and the upsweep.

Probably the most serious technical fault for swimmers is called *dropped elbow*. Since you apply more force when your elbow is above your hands during the downsweep and insweeps, dropped elbow reduces propulsion. Slower swimmers allow their elbow to drop lower in the water and travel backward in advance of their hands. The result of dropped elbow is a decrease in leverage of the arm that increases resistance to forward motion. Little propulsion is produced by a dropped-elbow stroking action.

Common Stroke Errors

"I already know how to swim," you're probably saying. Chances are, however, that your stroke mechanics could be improved, thereby increasing your efficiency and decreasing your time. Common mistakes that even strong swimmers make include:

- Overreaching when you enter the water, causing your hips and legs to be pulled out of alignment, or underreaching, which exerts a counterforce that reduces forward velocity.
- Entering the water with your hand in a prone position, which will increase drag.
- During the downsweep, turning the palm inward immediately upon entry, which reduces propulsion, or pushing down on the water with the palm, which causes the drag force to push your body upward and disrupt your horizontal alignment.
- When initiating the insweep, pitching the hand inward before it passes inside the shoulder line, which reduces propulsion from the downsweep, or failing to pitch the hand inward during the insweep.
- Wasting energy by using your arms over the water during recovery in a low, lateral manner that interferes with lateral alignment.
- Plunging the hands deeply, paddle-wheel fashion, the elbow only slightly bent, so that too much energy is wasted on downward and upward thrust.
- Tracking the arms underwater in paths right and left of the centerline or overrolling the arms across the centerline so that

much energy is wasted in sideward thrust. Remember to roll to the centerline.

- Angling the wrists inappropriately so that the hands' surface area is not maximized. Remember to hold the palm rearward.
- Sweeping the arms wide in a recovery so that the body flexes sideward in compensation, thus increasing resistance to forward motion. Remember to "buzz the ear" on the way to reentry.
- Breathing at the wrong moment in the stroke cycle so that the arms must hesitate for every gasp. Remember the air pocket created by forward motion and breathe during the stroke.
- Holding the head too high out of the water so that fluid flow is rougher. Remember to project the face only slightly to the front.
- Lunging through the stroke so that much energy is wasted on extreme resistance or coasting with the arms so that little force is generated. Concentrate on smooth stroke acceleration.

A faster turnover rate will, of course, result in greater speed. A powerful arm can thrust rapidly through the water, but the greater force of resistance at higher hand velocities will result in more rapid muscle fatigue. A triathlon swimmer who is working out to improve speed must practice thrusting quickly through the water while maintaining form. Many noncompetitive swimmers are content to slog along at ever-longer distances without stressing their muscles by churning the stroke faster. Both strong muscles and endurance conditioning are required for an open-water swim at triathlon distance.

Wear a Lycra-spandex racing suit for minimum drag, tight-fitting goggles, and perhaps also a fluorescent orange cap in the open water for safety. Open-water swimmers should develop a strong water polo–type stroke, because it is necessary to lift the head completely out of water every six to 10 strokes. An adequate breaststroke or backstroke is also important for times when your muscles cramp, your throat gags on salt water, or you are simply tired.

The most serious difficulty in open rough water is maintaining breathing cadence, for the wash of choppy waves often floods the air pocket formed by forward speed. Since most triathlons hold the swim portion in lakes or the ocean, always practice heads-up swimming in rough water with a paddleboard or a rowboat in accompaniment.

The Kick

In a long-distance swim the kick is less powerful than in a sprint. It does not add much propulsion, but it does keep the legs from dragging downward.

CYCLING

Cycling is a sport of extremes: simple to learn, yet difficult to master; easier than walking at slow speeds, yet totally exhausting at full power; physically simple, yet mechanically complex. First, let's unravel the myriad terms, such as *derailleur, bottom bracket,* and *downtube,* so that you can become familiar with the parts of your 10- or 12-speed. The diagram below is a guide for you to study and memorize, to give you a command of the jargon relating to frames and components. If you are unfamiliar with these key terms, spend some time memorizing them so that you can identify them easily.

Most of us learned to ride a bike in childhood, but for the best performances we need to refine certain techniques. Subtle changes in riding style can dramatically improve both your efficiency and your enjoyment. By practicing proper pedaling, braking, shifting, and riding positions, you can maximize your pedal power and more effectively glide over that pavement. Here are some suggestions on how to ride competitively.

Riding Position

Your 10-speed will have dropped handlebars. There are three

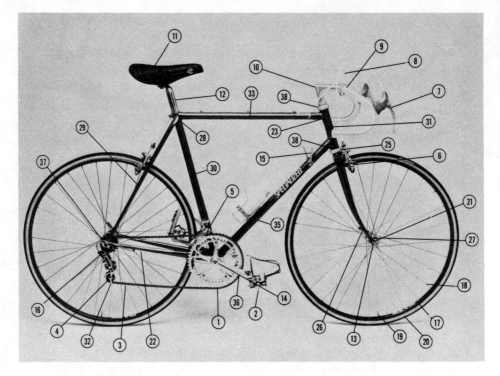

Key to Bicycle Parts

1. Chainwheel
2. Pedal
3. Chain
4. Rear derailleur
5. Front derailleur
6. Caliper brake
7. Brake lever
8. Brake cable
9. Handlebars
10. Handlebar stem
11. Seat (saddle)
12. Seat post
13. Quick-release skewer (for instant wheel removal)
14. Bottom bracket
15. Gear-shift lever for rear derailleur
16. Freewheel gear cluster
17. Rim
18. Spoke
19. Valve
20. Tire
21. Hub (high-flange type)
22. Chainstay
23. Lug
24. Fender
25. Fork crown
26. Fork
27. Front wheel dropout
28. Seat cluster lug
29. Seat stay
30. Seat tube
31. Head tube
32. Tension roller, rear derailleur
33. Top tube
34. Fender brace
35. Downtube
36. Cotterless crank
37. Rear wheel dropout
38. Headset (top and bottom)

basic hand positions on the bars, each providing different advantages.

1. The lowest position is with your hands on the hooks. This position results in the least wind resistance and the most effective posture for pulling uphill or for attaining high speeds. It also puts your body in the best alignment to maximize your muscle levers on the pedals, especially when using toe clips and racing shoes.

2. The highest position is with your hand on the top of the handlebars. This position is best for leisurely pedaling on flat roads. You encounter the greatest wind resistance this way because of the position of your body, but you are able to see better.

3. The compromise position is with your hands on the padded brake hoods. This position is called *riding the brakes* and combines good visibility and lower wind resistance. Change positions as you ride to cope with sore back muscles and numb hands.

To make sure that your bicycle is adjusted properly, place your hands on the hooks. As in the photo below, your line of sight should pass through the connection point between handlebar stem and handlebars to the wheel hub. You shouldn't be able to see the hub if the line of sight and the stem length are correct.

Turning

As you approach the turn, decide on a track and follow it without changing your mind (unless you are forced to because of obstructions or miscalculations). Brake before, not during, the turn. As you enter the turn, lean into it and slightly steer the handlebars. Most of the turning force will come from your body's angle, or *lean*. Raise your inside pedal to prevent it from scraping the ground. Point your inside knee toward the inside of the turn to aid your balance.

Proper adjustment for stem length.

Shifting

To shift a 10-speed properly, continue pedaling slightly, easing up on the pedal pressure a little as you shift. Never backpedal. If your shift-lever arms are mounted on the handlebar end, use your pinky to shift. If your levers are mounted on the downtube, put one hand over the center of the handlebars as you take your other hand off the handlebar to shift. Know this technique by feel; don't look down. If you hear a rattling sound after you shift, move the lever gently until the noise stops. A continuous jingling rattle means that your rear derailleur is out of position and that the chain is rubbing against the next-largest freewheel cog. An intermittent rasping rattle means that the chain is hitting the front derailleur during part of the pedaling cycle.

Anticipate the gear you will need next. Look ahead at the road grade and evaluate its slope and surface and the traffic conditions. Proper timing of the shift keeps your spin in perfect cadence. Otherwise you will be in the middle of a steep climb, losing speed drastically as you shift (and your chain may jump off the sprockets).

CHOOSING THE CORRECT GEAR To choose the proper gear you must know the chainwheel and freewheel gear (rear cluster) ratios of your bicycle. This information is easy to calculate and memorize. Follow the simple formula that follows:

1. Count the number of teeth on each of the front two chainwheels. Count the number of teeth on the rear five to seven cogs.

number of teeth on front chainwheel	Number of Teeth on the REAR COGs					Gear Number
	14	17	21	27	34	
52	100.3	82.6	66.9	52.0	41.3	6-10
40	77.1	63.5	51.4	40.0	31.8	1-5

My Ten-Speed Gear Chart.

	Number of Teeth on the REAR COGs					Gear Number
number of teeth on front chainwheel						
						6-10
						1-5

Your Ten-Speed Gear Chart.

2. Next, calculate the ratios of the different combinations, in *gear inches,* using this simple formula:

Gear inches = $\dfrac{\text{number of teeth on the front chainwheel} \times 27 \text{ inches (wheel diameter)}}{\text{number of teeth on the rear cog}}$

Example:

$\dfrac{52 \text{ (front chainwheel count)} \times 27 \text{ inches}}{14 \text{ rear cog teeth count}}$ = 100.3 gear inches

   The combination in this example is a high gear. Calculate all the combinations for the large chainwheel, then for the small chainwheel. As shown in Chart 1 below, list them in order, with gear 1 being low and 10 being high in Chart 2.

3. Eliminate the gears you should not use. The fact that you have a 10-speed does not mean that you have 10 useful gears. Cross out the big chainwheel/small rear cog combination and the small chainwheel/big rear cog combination in order to eliminate wear from a severely angled chainline. If you are buying a new bike, select the appropriate gear through the correct chainrings and freewheel cluster combination. Most dealers will be happy to accommodate your needs. Remember, get useful gears in evenly spaced intervals as much as possible. The highest gear that most people can comfortably push is in the 100–105 range, and the lowest gear you'll usually need is in the 36–40 range.

GEAR	COMBINATION	GEAR RATIO	DISTANCE TRAVELED (inches)	(Feet)	
1 (low)	40 x 34	31.8	100″	8.3′	(easiest to turn)
2	40 x 27	40.0	126″	10.5′	
3	40 x 21	51.4	161″	13.4′	
4	40 x 14	63.5	199″	16.6′	→overlap
5	~~40 x 14~~				eliminate due to chain line
6	~~52 x 34~~				
7	52 x 27	52.0	163″	13.6′	
8	52 x 21	66.9	210″	17.5′	
9	52 x 17	82.6	268″	22.4′	
10 high	52 x 14	100.3	315″	26.2′	(hardest to turn)

*gear ratio × 3.14 = distance traveled

My Bicycle Shift Sequence.

GEAR	COMBINATION	GEAR RATIO	DISTANCE TRAVELED (inches)	(Feet)	
1 (low)					(easiest to turn)
2					
3					
4					
5					eliminate due to chain line
6					
7					
8					
9					
10 high					(hardest to turn)

*gear ratio × 3.14 = distance traveled

Your Bicycle Shift Sequence.

4. Identify combinations that are similar. In the example charted, gears 3 and 7 are virtually identical, and gears 4 and 8 are very close. In actuality you have seven useful ratios out of the possible 10 combinations. Multiply each gear inch by *pi* (3.14) to find the distance traveled along the ground for each revolution of the crank in a given gear. The best way to learn the proper shift sequence is to memorize these combinations. Start by taping a copy of the gear plan to your toptube with waterproof tape.

5. Plan the proper shift sequence. The purpose of sequencing is to avoid using the front derailleur any more than necessary. For the gear range cited in the example, when climbing steadily up a variable grade, shift through the inner four cogs running off the small chainwheel. When on the flat against a variable wind, shift through the outer four cogs running off the large chainwheel. Think of your 10-speed as a 4-speed in low range and a 4-speed in high range.

Spinning

An important term in bicycling jargon is *spinning*—maintaining a rapid crank cadence. It is an essential technique for high performance because it reduces the brute force required to turn the crank. It simply is more efficient. You still must put out the same energy, but you divide it up over more repetitions. An analogy in weightlifting would be hefting a weight of 50 pounds in five reps rather than 250 pounds in only one. A skilled cyclist uses a pedal cadence of 60–100 revolutions per minute (rpm), maintaining this steady cadence on flats as well as up hills by changing gears to conform to the grade. By contrast, recreational cyclists turn only 40–60 rpm. In training, strength is built by starting out in gear 7 or 8 at a spinning cadence and overloading in progressively higher gears without slowing cadence. Resist the temptation to shift into high when you want to go faster. Be a spinner rather than a lugger.

Pedal Cadence

		Novice	Expert
Flat terrain,	gear inch—	66–68	70–75
light wind	cadence—	80 rpm	100 + rpm
Descents,	gear inch—	70–75	80–90
trail winds	cadence—	80 rpm	100+
Hills,	gear inch—	40–60	60
mountains	cadence—	50–60 rpm	60 rpm

Pedaling

One of the advantages of spinning is that the reduction in pedal force allows the legs' weaker pulling muscles to complement the powerful pushing muscles so that force is applied evenly throughout each revolution. This technique requires toe clips. Each leg exerts force through extension during the push phase and through retraction during the pull phase. Furthermore, force can be applied during the upper advance and lower retreat of the crankset through a technique called *ankling,* which requires cleated cycling shoes. Altogether, turning force can move in a complete circle, employing the various leg muscles equally. The result is greater propulsion with less strain.

Special Riding Situations

With a little experience you will learn the gear sequences and cadences that suit you for flat surfaces and gentle grades. Then there are the hills!

Excess weight—on you or your bike—really shows up on the hills. The best natural hill climbers have good power-to-weight ratios. In other words, they're built lean, and the weight they carry is mostly muscle. Apart from this, successful hill climbing comes from

Ardis Bow in the proper hill climbing position: hands on top of the brake calipers while standing on the pedals.

When descending a hill, keep your feet at the same level, tuck your elbows in, put your chin down next to the bars, and stick your butt up. Presto! A human wedge.

developed skill and hard work. You have to develop your strength and the technique that fits you.

Hill-climbing cadence is slower than the cadence for riding on level ground and slight grades. Normal cadence would be in the 60–80 rpm range, depending on the steepness of the hill and the gear in which you choose to attack it.

Most riders combine a technique of sitting in the saddle and standing on the pedals when they climb a hill. Sitting in the saddle works better for more moderate hills. If you use a lower gear and cadence, sitting back in the saddle and concentrating on the power you're transmitting to the pedals works better. If you use a higher

Dress for comfort and warmth when cycling.

gear and cadence, pull back on the bars as you pedal forward and downward, using your lower back muscles. (Keep your hands on top of the bars; there's no real aerodynamic advantage in going to the hooks with your hands.)

Changing positions in the saddle on long hills keeps your muscles fresher for a longer period of time because you are working them in different ways. When hills get steeper, you can go down a gear or two and stay in the saddle or you can get up on the pedals, another way to vary the load and keep your legs lively. This gives you the advantage of adding power to your stroke from your body weight. Here's where technique comes in. As you push down on a pedal (your hands are up on the brake levers) you pull up with the same arm. Your bike will sway from side to side; but if you keep tracking straight, you won't waste energy. Of course, if you want to ride hills well, you have to get out there and practice.

Downhills are fun, and, with the right technique, you can erase most of the risk and gain some time. First, anticipate a downhill by getting into high gear right at the crest of the hill you've just climbed. Use your legs to pedal for as long as you can, with your chin down over the headset and your hands on the drops. Then, when you can only coast, get your butt up high, bring your legs to the same height in the stroke, tuck in your elbows and knees, and fly! Anticipate the curves, brake only when you need to, and keep your front wheel in good shape. A flat under these circumstances could mean curtains.

Clothes

Experienced cyclists wear snug-fitting shorts without seams at any point where the bottom contacts the seat and tight jerseys to minimize wind resistance. Some triathletes have thought nothing of wearing loose jackets with food-stuffed pockets billowing in the wind like spinnakers. Inexperienced cyclists often suffer knee problems in cool weather because of wind chill. The knee has comparatively poor blood circulation and must be protected from heat loss, especially when the effective temperature drops by 20 degrees or more because of wind speed past the legs. Use leg warmers for colder conditions and, as for cold-weather running, dress in light layers. A layer of smooth, soft wool next to your skin will wick away water. On the surface, wear a nylon (or Gore-Tex, if you can afford it) windbreaker.

Mechanics

Keep the tire pressure up to the prescribed rating. A drop of 10–20 pounds may not be readily noticeable to the eye but can cost you speed. Seat and handlebar adjustments should be correct for optimum leg placement, the leg almost fully extended at the bottom of the stroke. Of course, the frame size should fit your body.

Keep your bike clean and lubricated, and it will reward you by not letting you down when you need it most. It's easier than you might think. A friend of mine has a gorgeous hand-made racer that he keeps spotless; the hubs gleam! I asked him how much time he spent cleaning his bike, and he said that he gave everything an initial four or five coats of car wax and now he just spends about five minutes twice a week wiping it off with a soft cloth. The parts that collect grit most frequently are both derailleurs, the chain, the brakes, and the lower ring of the headset. The chain is the only part that needs regular (once every week or two) lubrication. Motorcycle chain lube (aerosol) is good. WD-40, for example, is too light for the chain. Be sure to wipe off the excess, or your back wheel and clothing will catch it. Remember, it's just what reaches the internal parts of the chain that does any good.

Field Repairs

Bicycles are elegant but fairly simple machines. With a little study and practice you'll be able to do just about everything but true and build wheels. Pick up a good book that shows all the major systems disassembled. *Richard's Bicycle Book,* by Richard Ballan-

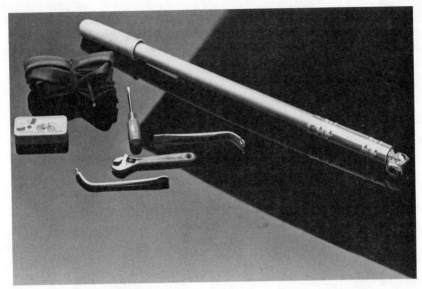

Basic tools required for tire repair.

tine (Ballantine Books, Inc., New York, 1982), is the best small book I've seen. Tom Cuthbertson's *Anybody's Bike Book: An Original Manual of Bicycle Repairs* (Ten Speed Press, Berkeley, 1979) is another good one.

The more you learn about how your bike works, the more confident you will be when you ride. Learn how all major systems—the driveline (freewheel, chain, chainrings, derailleurs, cranks, and pedals), brakes, headset, wheels, and hubs—work, and disassemble them just for fun.

If you keep your bike in good repair—maintain the cables and brake pads and keep all bolts tight—the only thing that's liable to let you down on a training run or in a race is the wheels. You'll break a spoke (not common) or get a flat tire (much more likely). You can use sew-up or clincher tires. Here are the pros and cons of each:

Sew-ups are more expensive, more efficient, easier to change, more difficult and expensive to repair, and somewhat more easily punctured. Clinchers are cheaper, slightly less efficient in terms of rolling resistance, harder to change, and relatively more durable.

If you have a choice (read: if you can afford it), you might consider buying two sets of wheels, one to race on and one to train on. Train on high-pressure clinchers and race on sew-ups. This makes sense only if you consider yourself a contender, and here's why you might want to do it: you can change a sew-up tire in about two minutes. You just whip off the old tire and slip on the new one. But it's hard to change a flat on a clincher in less than 10–15 minutes. You have to pull off one side of the tire, pull out the tube, patch or replace it, carefully fit it back in, and then replace the tire.

A good compromise might be to get a really strong set of sew-ups. I had a set of Clement Campionato del Mondos (silk) that lasted about 2,000 miles with no problems, and Wolber now makes a steel-belted sew-up that's very puncture-resistant and not too heavy (295 grams).

By the way, if you use clinchers, get *cloth* rim strips to cover the spoke holes, *not* rubber, which are the most common. It's easy for the tube to wedge its way into the spoke holes, get pinched, and *BAM!* Flat tire! At high speed, this could be *very* dangerous.

So, in your field repair kit (a small bag under or behind your seat), you will want to carry one or two tires (if you use sew-ups), a tube and patch kit, and perhaps a foldable clincher (Specialized's Turbo series folds easily) if you decide on clinchers, and a small crescent wrench, screwdriver, and spoke wrench. Tape a couple of spokes to the seat stays.

Safety

Bugproof glasses with a rearview mirror attached, padded leather gloves to cushion the grip and protect you from a fall, a hard helmet, reflectors on the bike and clothes, a headlight for night riding— none of these contribute to speed, but they could save you much grief, especially when you are just missed by a passing car.

Safety equipment: padded gloves, hard helmet, durable pants, and bug-proof glasses with rearview mirror attached.

RUNNING

Soon after learning to walk, you learned to run. The way you run is as much a motor set—a specific sequence of actions dictated by your movement memory—as is your handwriting. It is possible to identify friends in the distance, for example, simply by recognizing their running style. Nevertheless, it is possible for you to reprogram your running motor set, just as it is possible to develop a new handwriting pattern. Reprogramming takes practice, concentration, and the will to change. You must formulate an ideal style based on sound principles and compare yourself to that ideal, incrementally adjusting your form while evaluating results. One of the best methods is to study and then mimic the styles of good runners.

Julie Leach, October 1982 IRONWOMAN winner, at the end of the race when fatigue leads to poor running form—tilted head, high knees, misalignment of body.

Style

The ideal style for long-distance running can be analyzed by isolating the parts involved.

HEAD—Many runners have a tendency to fix their gaze on their feet. The result is rounded shoulders and bent hips. Often, runners will pull in their chins and tense their necks, like scared turtles. In order to use your full lung capacity it is best to look ahead approximately 30 feet, with your face directly over your base of support and your chest open.

UPPER BODY—Keep all swinging motion aligned with your running direction so that you won't roll around your central axis. Keep your shoulders square and straight ahead, with little swing.

ARMS—Keep your arms relaxed and free from tension. Your elbows should be cocked at a 90-degree angle and swung forward and back parallel to the direction in which you are running without crossing over your body's centerline.

HANDS—Keep your hands relaxed, cupped rather than clenched tightly.

HIPS—Sprinters lean forward at the hips so that their center of gravity leads their footplant. Distance runners are straighter at the hips, keeping their body weight centered above their footplant.

KNEES—One of the weak points of the body is the knee joint. It must be protected from abuse. Eliminate the high knee action that sprinters use to increase leg thrust. Distance runners glide low to the ground, thus decreasing the shock of landing hard.

FEET—Land on the outside of your heel and roll inward toward your big toe. The big toe is a two-jointed bone structure (all the other toes are three-jointed) and is well suited to bear the body's weight in the push-off. Rolling along the sole results in reduced muscle soreness and bone stress.

STRIDE LENGTH—By definition, the stride length is the distance between footfalls. It is increased by leg thrust, not by leg reach. Keep your footfall underneath you; don't try to step ahead. Increase your speed by thrusting at a fast cadence rather than by loping in a longer stride. The fastest marathoners are quick shufflers, whose legs flex only a little in a rapid turnover kept close to the ground. The overall power of the stride will be increased by minimizing the amount of power wasted in excessive vertical motion of the legs and body.

Common Gait Errors

Errors in running posture are not uncommon. First, it is necessary to analyze your gait pattern and then learn to make the necessary changes. There are several ways for you to analyze your technique. You can take photographs or videotape your style; you can watch your shadow or your image in large plate-glass windows when running downtown; you can ask a qualified individual to make observations. Regardless of which you choose, it is worth the time and expense to develop a kinesthetic sense of your running movement patterns. Here are some of the most common gait problems.

OVERSTRIDING—Overstriding is caused by extending the hip flexors in an attempt to eke out a few extra inches in the length of your stride. Instead, shorten the distance between footplants and move your arm swing slightly faster. This is best done by consciously shortening the stride of the forward-reaching foot.

INCORRECT KNEE LIFT—Lift the knees just high enough for the feet to clear the ground during the recovery phase. Concentrate on minimizing knee lift and thus save your energy.

ARMS TOO HIGH—By raising the arms above waistline height you are causing increased participation of your chest muscles, which are needed for respiratory functions. Keep the elbows close to the body with the palms of the hands inward and upward.

TIGHTNESS IN THE HANDS, ARMS, SHOULDERS—Concentrate on keeping the upper body loose. Practice using quick-step drills for warm-ups. By keeping your fingers loose you will be forced to relax your hands, arms, and shoulders.

BOUNCING TOO HIGH—This can be eliminated through lower knee lift, leaving the foot in contact with the ground longer after it passes under your center of gravity. Try using a reaching action with the arms rather than a pumping action.

LANDING ON YOUR HEELS—There is a tendency to land on mid-foot the when running faster. Shortening the stride slightly will help.

BREATHING—Open all breathing orifices and inhale and exhale rhythmically and steadily. If this is difficult, set up a breathing pattern—a two-count beat. Exhale every second time the right foot strikes the ground.

RESISTANCE TRAINING

Since swimming, bicycling, and running are primarily aerobic sports, why include a section on resistance (weight) training? For two reasons. According to Ed Burke, an exercise physiologist and former competitive cyclist who has written for *Velo-News,* a bicycle racing journal, research has shown that there is a significant relationship between muscular endurance and maximum strength. In other words, if you train to increase your strength, your muscular endurance will increase. For those persons who consider themselves contenders for top finishing positions in triathlons, weight training could provide a competitive edge.

A minimal program is presented here. It is assumed that most of your training time is going to be spent in running, bicycling, or swimming workouts, so this plan is a series of the one or two best exercises for each major muscle group. This routine will take about a half hour and should be done three times a week; don't do weight workouts on consecutive days. I recommend doing it on days that you have easy aerobic workouts. To some degree it is assumed that you have (or can get) access to resistance equipment. There are three ways to go:

1. You can do resistance exercises in which your own weight provides the resistance, such as push-ups.
2. You can use free weights (barbells and dumbbells, which are inexpensive).
3. You can use machines (Nautilus and Universal Gym, for example), which are expensive, efficient, and available at YMCA-YWCAs, junior colleges, and health clubs.

Here is the way to figure out whether you have enough resistance (weight) in a particular exercise: you should be able to do eight to 10 repetitions of the exercise before the muscle group that you are exercising becomes totally fatigued, and you should do each exercise to the point of failure (i.e., until you can't do another rep). If you reach failure before eight reps, take off some weight; if you do 12–15 reps, put some weight on.

A *repetition,* as you may have gathered, is one complete performance of an exercise. A *set* is a group of repetitions. Unless you have very good muscle tone, do one set of each exercise for the first two weeks, then move up to two sets and remain there.

These exercises will develop muscle strength, tone, definition and, necessarily, *size* and *weight.* Only develop your muscles to the extent that is functionally useful to you. That means, in practice, that once you've developed your routine, add resistance (i.e., put on more weight) to a particular exercise when it becomes easy to do. In general, do an exercise at a given resistance for a couple of weeks and add weight in increments of five to 10 pounds. When you're as strong or as developed as you want to be, keep the weight at that level. The principle is the same as in aerobic training.

The normal procedure when working with weights is to do a set of exercises, wait a minute or two for your muscles to recover, and then repeat the set. If you want to save time, you might consider going immediately on to another exercise that exercises an opposing or completely different muscle group instead of resting. A word

Crunch.

of caution: when working with heavy weights (especially free weights), be careful. If you're doing bench presses with (heavy) free weights, have a friend with you who can spot you (i.e., pull the weight off your chest or neck) in an emergency.

Stomach

Stomach muscles are good muscles to exercise for general warming up. The first two exercises, sit-ups and crunches, work the front abdominals.

BENT-LEG SIT-UPS: If you haven't done stomach exercises for a while, start off by doing standard bent-leg sit-ups. Sit on the floor (on a pad or comfortable carpet, so that you don't bruise your tailbone), bend your legs at the knees, and hook your feet under a couch or have a friend hold them down. Clasp your hands together behind your head and lower yourself to the floor, keeping your back as straight as possible. Lift yourself so that your trunk is vertical (you don't need to touch your elbow to your knee), keeping your back straight, for one repetition. Start with one set of 10–15 sit-ups, and work up to one set of 25. Be sure to breathe frequently in this exercise.

CRUNCH: After two weeks of regular sit-ups you'll be ready to move on to the most effective and efficient stomach exercise, the crunch. One way to do it is to assume the same position as for the bent-leg sit-up; but when you lift yourself up (back straight), stop about halfway, or where the tension is the greatest, tuck your chin in toward your chest, and pull with the muscles in the back of your neck. Hold the position until your stomach muscles fail. Repeat five to 10 times. Work up to 10–15 seconds per crunch.

SIDE BEND: This is another excellent abdominal exercise. Stand looking straight ahead and place your feet about one foot apart. Hold a dumbbell (15–30 pounds) in one hand and hang it straight down at your side. Bend from the side and try to reach as far as you can down the side of your leg with your empty hand, fingers pointed. Try to feel the pull in the muscles at the side of your waist, which this exercise develops. Do 25 reps, change sides, and repeat.

Chest

BENCH PRESS: The best single exercise for development of the chest muscles (pectorals) is the bench press, which requires barbell or dumbbells and a weight bench. Or you can do ordinary military push-ups or use a Universal Gym or Nautilus machine. Only the bench press is explained here because the basic muscular motion is the same in all three.

Lie flat on your back on a weight bench with a barbell on the weight rack in front of your face. Reach up and grasp the barbell with your hands at about shoulder width, lift it off the rack, and lower it to your chest. Raise it vertically to full arm extension for one repetition. Work up to two sets of 10 repetitions. You can do the same exercise with dumbbells.

Bench Press.

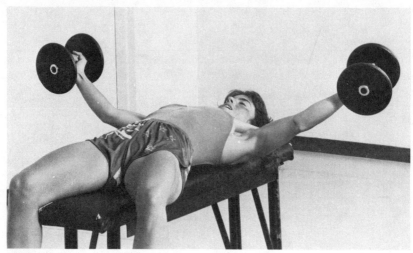

Dumbbell Flyes.

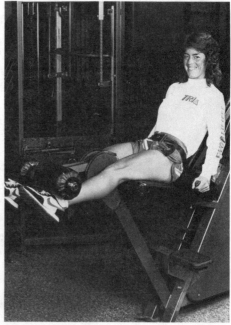

Leg Extension—start, left; finish, right.

DUMBBELL FLYES: For this exercise, lie on your back on the weight bench, a dumbbell in each hand, held vertically (perpendicular to your body). Lock your elbows and turn your palms inward, bringing the dumbbells together. Keeping your elbows stiff, lower the dumbbells straight out to each side until your hands are just below bench level, palms up. Raise the bells up for one repetition. Work up to two sets of 10 repetitions.

Legs

There are two good exercises for the thigh muscles: one for the quadriceps (front) and one for the biceps (back). Both require the use of a Nautilus, Universal Gym machine or an appropriate weight bench. In both exercises, move your legs slowly and deliberately; don't let the weight clank at the bottom of the stroke. Work for continuous, smooth motion. Build up to two sets of twelve repetitions.

LEG EXTENSION: The exercise for the quadriceps is the leg extension. Sit on the bench with your legs over the end, hook your ankles under the padded bars of the leg extension machine, and hold yourself firmly in place with your hands at the side of the bench. Straighten your legs (either together or one at a time, depending on the machine) against the resistance of the padded bar until they are nearly straight out in front of you. Lower for one repetition.

LEG CURL: The leg curl (for the biceps) requires you to lie face down on the bench and hook the back of your ankles below the upper padded bar of the machine. Holding yourself flat, curl your legs to bring your feet as close to your rear end as possible.

CALF LIFTS: For calves, the best single exercise is a calf lift of some kind. Calves and abdominals require heavy work—"bombing"—to really develop them, so doing three sets of 15–20 reps of calf raises is not excessive. Place the fronts of your feet on the edge of a telephone book or board about two or three inches thick. Place

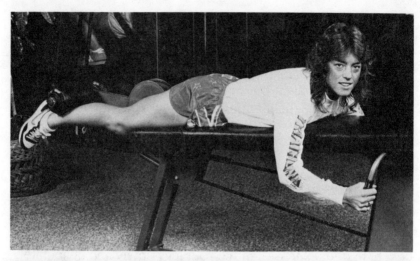

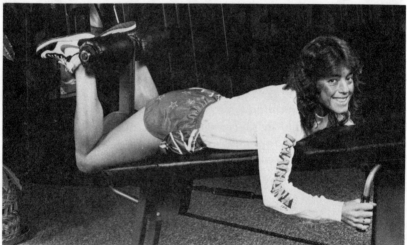

Leg Curl—start, top; finish, bottom.

a heavy dumbbell in one hand, support yourself by holding on to a pole or a chair with your other hand, and rise up as high as you can on your toes. Go for the greatest possible range of motion. When your calves "burn," you'll know you're getting a good workout.

Bent-Over Rowing—start, left; finish, right.

Back

BENT-OVER ROWING: Bent-over rowing can be used to strengthen the muscles of the upper back, called the latissimus dorsi. Rowing can be done with either a barbell or dumbbells. Place your feet about shoulder width apart, bend at the knees and waist, and reach down and grasp the barbell in an overhand grip, with your hands also about shoulder width apart. Come up until your torso is parallel with the floor, bent at the waist, arms extended straight down. Keep your knees slightly bent and make sure you don't put the strain on your lower back.

Stay bent over and lift the weight up to your lower chest, as if you were pulling oars. Feel the lift in your lats. Then lower the bar (or dumbbells), but not to the floor. Do two sets of 10 repetitions.

Military Press with dumbbells—start, left; finish, right.

Shoulders

MILITARY PRESS: For the shoulders (deltoids), the single best exercise is the standard *military press,* done with either a barbell or dumbbells. This exercise also works the back and triceps. Stand with the barbell on the floor in front of you, with your feet shoulder width or slightly farther apart. Bend down and grasp the bar in an overhand grip, straighten your legs and back, and in a continuous motion, pull the bar to shoulder height. Next tuck your elbows in so they are directly under the bar and the bar is supported just above your chest. Then push (don't jerk) the bar upward and lock your arms. From this position, with the weight balanced, lower the bar (or dumbbells) back to the shoulder for one repetition. Work up to 10 reps, two sets. It isn't necessary to lower the bar to the floor again until you are finished with all the reps. Again, don't cheat by thrusting the bar up rapidly. A good variation on this, which works the back of the deltoids, is to lower the bar behind your neck.

*Dumbbell Curl done
slightly bent and curling
out in front of the torso.*

Arms

DUMBBELL CURLS: The best basic exercise for the front of the
arm (biceps) is the curl, which can be done with the barbell but
is better done with dumbbells, because you tend to favor the weak
arm with barbells. Stand up straight with a dumbbell in each hand,
palms out, feet shoulder width apart. Lean your arms out a little
away from your body and alternately curl them toward your
shoulder. The value of the curl is seriously diminished once you
get past midpoint on the curl; you can feel it get easier. You can
overcome the effect of gravity by bending over a little and lifting
your elbow, moving your arm in an arc, so that at the top of the
curl, you're still pulling upward. Don't sling the bells around.
Rather, pull from the bicep all through the exercise. Do two sets
of 10 repetitions.

Dumbbell Tricep Extension—start, left; finish, right.

DUMBBELL TRICEP EXTENSION: For the triceps, there is a reasonably good exercise you can do with a dumbbell. Stand with your feet comfortably apart and hold a dumbbell with both hands over your head, elbows pointed forward. Extend your arms fully, hold your upper arms rigid and let the dumbbell drop behind your head, as if your elbows were hinges (which, in fact, they are). Raise the bell back up for one repetition. Be careful not to hit the back of your neck, and remember to keep your arm relatively stiff. Do two sets of 10.

#   #   #

Finally cool down with a set of 10 crunches or two sets of 25 bent-leg sit-ups.

A number of excellent books are available on bodybuilding. I highly recommend *Arnold's Bodyshaping for Women* (Simon & Schuster, New York, 1979) and *Arnold's Bodybuilding for Men*

(Simon & Schuster, New York, 1981), both by Arnold Schwarzenegger; *Staying Hard,* by Charles Gaines and George Butler (Simon & Schuster, New York, 1980); *Lisa Lyons' Body Magic*, by Lisa Lyons and Douglas K. Hall (Bantam Books, Inc., New York, 1981); and *The Gold's Gym Weight Training Book,* by Bill Dobbins and Ken Sprague (Berkeley Publishing Corp., New York, 1980).

SUMMARY

Recently, when training in the public pool in California, my friend and I found ourselves swept into a rhythm of identical strokes. Swimming in the adjacent lane, she would at times nudge ahead. In response I noticed that my inner voice would say, "Swimming form—sweep, glide, reach." As if motivated by the words, my efficiency improved; we would again be parallel, flip turn for flip turn. It was as if by concentrating on the mechanics of the motion, stressing the mental requirement to pay attention to the quality of my movement, not just the power, I could perform with greater ease.

Yes, when you are truly fine-tuned, your engine will work in coordination with your mental muscle in perfect harmony.

11

feeding the fires

"We have shown that there are definite ways to improve performance: carbohydrate loading, hyperhydration, sugar ingestion during long events, caffeine ingestion, and—most importantly—a well-balanced diet consisting mostly of complex carbohydrate."—Ellen Coleman, *Eating for Endurance,* 1980

The question invariably asked by people interested in health and fitness is "What is the best diet? What combination of fuels will best clean out my pipes, rev up the engines, and fire the motor that takes me through the rigorous physical and mental demands of my day?" Academic experts, health faddists, and successful experienced athletes expound at length on the subject, bombarding the American public with a mass of conflicting theories and recommendations. It is no wonder that we are confused.

Optimum diet can be defined as that particular combination of foods that stimulates the body to perform with maximum comfort and efficiency in a predictable variety of situations. A well-balanced diet should be a must for everyone, but it is of particular importance for those individuals in unusually stressful situations; e.g., the triathlete. How can we gauge the relative values of different food types in this search to find the best fuel? We can learn, perhaps, by the example of another culture.

The Hunzas, who live in the Karakoram Mountain Range of the Himalayas in Pakistan, count 2,875 centenarians per million, while the ratio of centenarians in the United States is only eight per

These are the basic foods that meet the requirements of living foods.

million, the lowest in the world. Furthermore, the Hunzas exist apparently cancer-free, according to a recent study by the United Nations' Educational, Scientific, and Cultural Organization (UNESCO). They work strenuously in an agricultural community, eating a diet that has been relatively unchanged for centuries. The Hunzas eat nuts, fruits, vegetables, and a variety of whole grains. Preservatives, additives, processing procedures, and chemicals have no place in the Himalayan diet, nor do meat and refined sugar. Although it would be simplistic to attribute the society's unusually high level of wellness to diet alone, it is clear that good nutrition and exercise have played a significant role in producing generations of healthy, vital, long-lived Hunzas.

Despite the diversity of their individual theories, health experts generally agree on one basic formula for good health:

$$\begin{aligned}
&\text{Balanced nutrition}\\
&+ \text{ exercise}\\
&+ \text{ sleep}\\
&+ \text{ fresh air}\\
&+ \text{ good genes}\\
&+ \text{ moderate exposure to sunlight}\\
\hline
&= \text{ the best chances for good health.}
\end{aligned}$$

The Hunza society is a living testament to this; the core of their nutritional program might well be adapted to the programs of other active individuals. If the body is a temple, as the great teachers say, we shouldn't treat it as if it were a motel.

Serious triathletes should carefully monitor the amount, type, and nutritional value of the foods they ingest. The diet that is probably optimum for an endurance athlete is one that will both tune up the engine and turn it on to high performance. The human body is an incredible energy machine. It needs and demands foods that will fuel it accordingly. I have found a simple set of criteria that helps me unravel the confusion caused by obsolete theories, commercial interests, disagreement among experts, and the lack of reliable information. I simply ask the question *"What will it give me, and what will it cost me?"*

Food gives the body a source of fuel that it can burn for energy, plus certain nutritional benefits (e.g., protein to repair muscle tissue). On the other hand, food can cost the body. It may provide empty (relatively nonnutritious) calories, or it may be difficult and/or take a lot of time to digest. So, to use an economic metaphor, there is a cost/benefit ratio that applies to the act of eating. It only makes sense, therefore, that we require that the food we put into our incredible machines pay some dividends—that it give us more than it costs us.

As you become fine-tuned you will probably notice that your body begins to regard food as the fuel that makes those muscles operate efficiently. Muscle burns primarily glucose and glycogen. We know that 90 percent of all calories burned in a day's activities are consumed by the muscle tissues. It would seem reasonable, then, to feed our muscles those fuels that they can make the best use of—carbohydrates, which are the source of muscle sugars.

That is what I eat. I eat to feed my muscles, which eat carbohydrates. I do not eat to feed fat, since my body already contains sufficient amounts of fat without encouraging it to multiply. Protein, needed to rebuild or resynthesize tissues, is required only in small quantities. If we break down the three principal food sources in terms of calories ingested, I use the following formula as my guide:

75 percent of total calories in complex carbohydrates
10 percent of total calories in protein
15 percent of total calories in fat

I am often asked if I eat meat. Meat, whether red or otherwise, is something that I avoid. Let's apply the cost/benefit criteria to meat—what will it give and what will it cost? Meat gives protein and fat but no carbohydrates. The costs? Meat is high in chemicals (adrenaline and uric acid from slaughterhouse shock). Meat also takes a great deal of digestive time and is high in calories. Consequently, meat fails the test—too many costs for the benefits derived.

TIPS ON NUTRITION

Here are a few everyday nutritional guidelines that I follow:

1. Eat whole foods. This means foods that are complete, unfragmented, unrefined, neither fortified nor enriched. Fill up your grocery cart with spinach, nuts, lettuce, rice, barley, and so on.

2. Eat complex carbohydrates. These are the foods that form the gasoline that fires up our motors—grains, breads, potatoes. They digest more slowly than simple sugars—cookies, ice cream, cake—and do not produce a rapid rise and fall in blood-sugar level.

3. Eat modest amounts of protein. The old-time nutritionists said, "Eat what you are made of." Nutritionists today say, "Eat what gives you energy—carbohydrates."

4. Eat living foods. Such foods as apples, bananas, carrots, sunflower seeds, and sprouts are considered living foods because they are in their original state.

5. Eat unprocessed foods. These are foods with no chemicals, preservatives, or sweeteners added, those that have not been altered mechanically or by cooking or freezing. Avoid chemical additives. Apply this simple test: If you can't wash it, don't eat it.

6. Eat unpackaged foods. Canned, jarred, sealed, or frozen food must be adulterated for containment.

7. Eat foods in combination. To assimilate and digest foods optimally, present them to your stomach in balanced combination.

8. Eat to feed your muscles, not your fat. Eat only as much as you need, not as much as you might want. Fat is nonworking tissue, so there is no need to feed it.

9. Eat balanced calories. Divide your calories among protein (10 percent), fat (15 percent), and carbohydrates (75 percent)—your three food sources.

Here are some additional tips about food and eating.

- It sometimes aids digestion to eat only one food or one type of food at a meal. For example, you might want to eat one or two potatoes or a vegetable. Eat simply.

- Chew your food well. The saliva in your mouth begins the chemical breakdown of the food; this is the start of the digestive process.

- Be sure you *breathe* while you chew; it will enhance the flavor and contribute to overall satisfaction. As a result, you may find that you don't eat as much.

- Eat in a relaxed, pleasant environment. Don't combine eating with loud, disruptive activities such as animated conversation or noisy music. Concentrate on and enjoy the process of eating.

- Be aware of how nutrients in food are easily lost. Eat fresh foods and cook them lightly, if at all.

- Remember, there is no need to eat *meals* as such, three times a day, at conventional times. Let *real* hunger be a guide to *when* and *how much* you eat.

- If you wish to lose weight, eat very little food after 6:00 P.M. Since you are less likely to be physically active then, the chances are greater that any food you eat will be stored as fat.

Food Supplements

One of the areas of heated debate with regard to the American diet today is the question of food supplements. Some people feel that if you eat three balanced meals a day, you will receive all of the MDR (minimum daily requirements) of vitamins, minerals, and other nutrients needed by the body. On the other hand, the pill industry lobbies fiercely to raise those MDR levels and to get you to feel that you must swallow a one-a-day vitamin.

As an endurance athlete, I frequently stress my incredible energy machine to its capacity. Then I demand that my immune system resist breakdown and rebuild my body to higher levels of work capacity. This stress-and-rebuild regimen requires more from my system than the average American requires. Average Americans lead a sedentary life. They inflict on themselves toxins such as cigarette smoke, overindulgence in alcohol, and packaged/canned/ "fast" foods. They lack stress reducers (hobbies, exercise, etc.) and have difficulty pushing themselves away from the television set or from a second helping at dinner.

It seems logical that the minimal daily nutritional requirements for the average American and the endurance athlete would be different. I use my body for physical performance, while many people use it to house their indulgences. Pose the nutritional test: *What will it give me and what will it cost me?* Intake of food supplements above the MDR passes the nutritional test. The benefits are to strengthen the immune system and the costs are the price of the supplements. Is it worth it? Probably.

Listen to your body and keep a nutritional performance journal. If a food or vitamin improves your performance, use it; if not, don't.

Your diet is one of the few variables that you can control. It is worth the expenditure in time to maximize the benefits by eating intelligently.

EATING FOR PERFORMANCE

While your arms are thrusting through the water or your legs spinning down the road or your feet racing toward the finish line, your stomach is (1) quiet, (2) hungry, (3) upset, (4) in contraction, or (5) in the unpleasant process of emptying itself. What your stomach can handle, other people's stomachs might not be able to. Some athletes advocate fasting or taking only fluids for the 24 hours before competition to cleanse the digestive tract and bowels. Some preach carbohydrate loading; some recommend eating steaks; some stoke up on waffles.

Carbohydrate Loading

There has been considerable controversy over the term

Eat to win.

carbohydrate loading. It's important for athletes to realize that there are two different kinds of loading.

Simple loading means increasing the amount of carbohydrates in your diet for several days before a big race.

Depletion loading is an involved procedure in which you first avoid dietary carbohydrates for a period of time while you continue your triple workouts. Then you switch fuels several days prior to the event to a high-carbohydrate diet.

A description of the carbohydrate-loading system was first published in 1966 as the result of the research of two Swedish physiologists. Their work showed that the depletion-loading procedure successfully gives athletes higher-than-normal muscle glycogen levels and significantly improved endurance.

As with other nutritional issues, you must apply the significant criteria and ask the important question "What will it give me, and what will it cost me?" There is no disagreement among the researchers as to whether the depletion-loading procedure increases levels of muscle glycogen. During the depletion phase you are essentially starving yourself of carbohydrates. This typically causes some starvation to the brain, because carbohydrates are its only fuel source. There can be unpleasant side effects of the depletion phase: insomnia, nervous tension, continual tiredness, irritability, and an inability to concentrate.

After the depletion phase you start to load carbohydrates. A new condition can now arise called *glycogen deposition disease.* Muscle glycogen is deposited inside the muscle as tiny granules much like little grains of sand. Glycogen deposition disease occurs when you overload the muscles with these small, sandlike granules, and they actually begin to disrupt the working muscle cells, causing painful muscle injuries.

The question of cost versus benefit in reference to loading is complicated by the fact that even if you survived the difficulties of depletion and accomplish significant glycogen loading without injury or mental deprivation, it is good for one shot at success. The physiological penance that you will pay to Mother Nature is great. And for what? How much improved performance time can you gain from this procedure? No one really knows. It *is* known that it will take several weeks to several months for you to restore the body's normal glycogen deposition capability after an exhausting endurance contest. During this recovery time you are guaranteed that your performances will be subnormal.

In deciding whether to depletion-load, I weigh the importance of the race. Knowing that the race must be more than two to three hours in duration for this procedure to be beneficial, I realize that there will be only a few races in a year's time that meet these requirements. Knowing that the carbohydrate depletion procedure is difficult to withstand, I select *the* key race (only one in a 12-month period), and I start loading six to eight days before the race. For three days I train hard in order to exhaust my body's stores of carbohydrates—"carbs" for short. During these three days I limit my carb consumption while I continue training, eating about 1,200 calories *each* of fat and protein per day. My consequent lethargy is a sure sign that the depletion of carbs in my system is taking place.

Nevertheless, I continue to train. Abruptly, three days before the race, I change both the fuels I eat and my exercise routine. I eat mostly carbs for the last three days and train only lightly. During this final period I might be eating 2,500 calories of complex carbs and 500 calories of fat and protein. The result is that my muscles become loaded with glycogen.

A triathlete practicing loading techniques must apply Commandment 6 (Specificity). The body stores glycogen only in the specific muscle groups that are exercised. Therefore, you must swim, run, and bicycle during these glycogen unloading and loading periods so that the muscle groups involved in these three sports deplete and reload their stores of glycogen. Some athletes and nutritionists believe that you don't need to follow the depletion phase, but only to ingest a high percentage (and greater amount) of carbohydrates the last three days before the race. In addition, there are some reports that it can be dangerous to use the program more than once or twice a year, so save it for the big competition.

PRERACE MEAL

The prerace meal must be composed of foods that you can keep in your gastrointestinal tract on a swim. If some people have food in their stomach during exercise, they suffer nausea (blood is sent to the working muscles and not the gut), impaired breathing, flatulence, or diarrhea. I train with food in my stomach to teach my digestive system to operate during exercise. Inevitable prerace nervousness slows down the digestive process somewhat.

Experiment and find out which foods sit best in your stomach. Generally, I eat two hours before the start of the longer races—a light, complex-carbohydrate meal of about 500–700 calories. I drink no milk within 48 hours of the race. Examples of food for the prerace meal are whole-grain cereal and whole-grain toast, pancakes, and juice. Foods with a high protein content are generally a bad choice since they remain in the stomach a long time. This pretriathlon meal needs to be substantial enough to eliminate both weakness and hunger. Eating two hours prior to the race insures that the stomach and upper bowels are relatively empty (I drink a cup of coffee at this time to help move my bowels along).

DURING-THE-RACE MEALS

For triathlons that last longer than three hours, eating during the race is as important as eating before the race. My criteria for what is acceptable food to eat during performance follow.

1. It must be unseasoned, low in fat, and free of dairy products.
2. It must be easy to chew.
3. It must digest relatively slowly and provide me with a trickle and not a flood of calories.
4. It must taste good.
5. It must not be monotonous.
6. It must not cause bowel trouble.
7. It must not bring on dehydration (it must be low in salts).
8. It must be able to be assimilated rapidly, so that my muscles can make use of the energy and liquid.

I know that what I eat during the race can contribute substantially to my performance. Realizing that, I want to store my glycogen and begin a fat metabolism cycle as early as possible (the reason for training moderately on some days). I even repeat to myself a nutritional mantra: "Burn fat, burn fat, burn fat."

Of course, I don't start eating until I am out of the water and on my bike. The foods that work best for me are pulped fruits (bananas, apples, or strawberries—my favorite). They can be packaged easily and swallowed quickly, and they meet all my criteria: variety, flavor, chewability, complex carbohydrates, easy on the stomach, a little difficult on the bowels.

After experimentation I have found that it is easier on the gastrointestinal tract to eat small amounts frequently rather than large amounts infrequently. I eat one-half cup of pureed fruits every half hour. I supplement this energy source with a hard rock candy that dissolves slowly in my mouth (seven minutes for a small piece). This gradual intake of calories helps to minimize the massive changes in blood-sugar level that occur with high-intensity exercise, and it reduces the pancreas's response to dumping insulin into the body in massive amounts. Slowly sucking on hard candy is similar to having an intravenous tube in your arm, slowly secreting small amounts of sugar into your system.

Some triathletes perform well during the ultrarace eating special liquid meals. Liquid meals were originally developed for hospital patients unable to eat solid foods. They are high in calories, provide for hydration, and are easily ingested. Do not confuse them with instant powdered meals or meal supplements, as these are generally mixed with milk and are high in fat and protein. Liquid meals are convenient, easily digested, soothing to a nervous stomach, high in carbs, and low in fats. Some brand name liquid diets are ENSURE (Ross Laboratories), SustaCal and Sustagen (Mead Johnson Laboratories), and Nutriment. Or you can make your own concoction and not have to worry about additives.

On a bike the stomach rides smoothly, but hands needed for eating are otherwise occupied. While running, the hands are free, but the stomach bounces. During extremely hot-weather races, watermelon is my favorite. It should be refrigerated, seeded, and cut into bite-sized pieces. Cantaloupe, strawberries, and other fruits in season excite my appetite. Also, I have found that certain cookies and sandwiches can be eaten easily.

The issue of whether to take aspirin during performance must be answered individually. I have found that aspirin helps my performance. It decreases minor pain and reduces swelling and inflammation in my joints. I have also found that too much aspirin or vitamins during exercise upset my stomach and decreased performance. You must experiment. If you have this problem, buffered aspirin might help. Some endurance athletes take caffeine tablets to receive the supposed benefit of caffeine: the release of free-floating fatty acids into the bloodstream for energy.

Fueling the fire: liquid replacement with an electrolyte-glucose drink.

FLUIDS

An athlete's need for fluids on a given day is highly individual. Hyperhydration is a practice I follow in hot-weather racing conditions. If you are hyperhydrated, you should weigh more on the morning of a race. During the race, fluid intake is crucial. The quantities you drink depend on weather, course conditions, and the sport. As a rule of thumb, I try to drink at least eight ounces of water every 15–30 minutes. After years of self-testing, I have found that I prefer water to commercial drinks. Other factors that determine your fluid requirements are your ability to sweat (those who sweat a great deal must drink more fluids) and the relative humidity (as the humidity increases, your ability to be cooled by sweating decreases). Water poured over the body during the race will help cool you. If the course lacks shade, your need for replacement fluids increases. Wearing a hat with a bill will keep you cool. Wearing white clothing will help, too. Drinking chilled fluids will also help lower your core (body) temperature—but take care, because cold liquids can give some people severe abdominal cramps.

It is best to take water on a schedule rather than waiting until you feel thirsty. The body's hydrostat doesn't always tell you how much you need. As with food, fluid is better taken more frequently in smaller amounts rather than less frequently in larger amounts. How much and how often you drink depends entirely on your own needs, your ability to utilize fluids, your body size, and the ambient temperature and humidity. When I train in the heat I carry a handheld 250-milliliter water bottle. On long runs I fill it frequently. During the race I take water at every aid station (at least four to six fluid ounces) and hope that the stations are spaced about 20 minutes apart. To cool my "radiator," I pour water over my head, always dancing in the process to avoid spillage on my Nikes.

As part of the here-and-now system check that I take during competition, I always ask myself for a readout on my stomach condition and my thermal states. To avoid the onset of tremendous fatigue it is important to try to keep up your blood-sugar level and maintain your fluid intake. If you have a need to urinate at least once every three hours, you are hydrated and your kidneys are still operating. Occasionally you might sense surges of high energy and good feelings, alternating with long periods of being down and feeling really bad. This condition is generally related to irregular calorie intake or assimilation.

All too frequently we see race organizers accepting beer companies as both sponsors and suppliers of postrace refreshments for the competitors. It is important for both the medical folks and the contestants to realize that the worst fluids possible at the conclusion of the race are those that contain alcohol in any significant percentage. Beer or any other beverage containing alcohol suppresses the antidiuretic hormone, the hormone responsible for controlling the water retention level in your bloodstream. The paralysis of the antidiuretic hormone causes you to dehydrate further by encouraging your kidneys to absorb blood fluids.

Remember that even though beer drinking may be lauded for its vitamin and mineral concentration, it is a disaster to your system's ability to rehydrate.

At the end of the race, the body needs fluids and rest. Water is absorbed faster than any other fluid (juice takes about 20 minutes to be absorbed). If the weather is particularly hot and dry, you will need to drink about two to three glasses of water. Then slowly drink some fruit juice. The water will replace lost blood volume; the juice will replace lost electrolytes (sodium, potassium, magnesium, calcium). Next, do some heavy-duty resting. Massage will help, as will hot baths.

CONCLUSION

Many superathletes feed their fires with junk food and still win races. They believe that the body is a garbage disposal, that when foods are broken down the body will take what it needs and eliminate the rest. Some even succeed with this philosophy. These athletes conclude that speed, strength, and stamina—not carrots—make champions.

I take a different position. I feel that we owe ourselves the best. If we're not willing to settle for junk living, we certainly shouldn't settle for junk food. As I've said, we need to take a hard look at our eating habits, find out what works, and adapt it. That's where it begins.

The next consideration (and, in the long run, the most important) is health. For me, health is much more than merely the absence of disease. It is a positive state of being that pervades our minds and bodies, enabling us to live long, productive, active, and energetic lives. The food we eat should make a positive contribution to that state of being. Eating, like everything else, should be an integral part of life. That's what this book is about—making sport (and nutrition) second nature, not just an afterthought in our lives.

Finally, we should consider performance. We should always try to do our best, but the years of our lives during which we're highly competitive are relatively few. But for those few peak years and special races, again, we owe it to ourselves to act on the best information available to us, and we should put the best possible fuel in our incredible energy machine. Socrates said that other men lived to eat while he ate to live. Perhaps you should improve on this maxim by saying, "Other men eat to live, while I eat to perform."

12

survival of the fit

"Fitness, like love, is finding your way back to yourself."

Fitness has its risks. A body in motion possesses high energy, which can be focused in a moment on bone or tissue with traumatic results—a tendon ripped from the inside, a skull fractured from the outside. The survival of the fit is a matter of taking wise precautions. Athletes are not guaranteed good health; they have to secure it with good sense.

Athletic activities can be dangerous, but statistics are somewhat misleading. A Consumer Products Safety Commission report cites 1,677,000 bicycle injuries in 1979. With almost 70 million Americans claiming to ride bicycles regularly, this amounts to only a 2.4-percent injury rate. Furthermore, three-quarters of bicycle injuries are suffered by children. Nonetheless, bicyclists, runners, and swimmers can be hurt by external or internal factors. Because a highly trained athlete is continually working at the edge of human capability, a crash or breakdown is not only always possible, it can be devastating.

STRESS INJURIES

You improve your strength and endurance as a result of stressing your body. Stress is a deliberate, controlled breakdown of tissue that results, with proper rest, in *adaptation,* or healing at a higher level of capability. If muscles are not allowed to rest until they repair

Julie Moss on the last stage of the IRONMAN triathlon as fatigue sets in.

themselves, their breakdown can be cumulative. This violation of Commandment No. 5 (Stress and recuperation) is called over-training. As you progress in triathlon training you will be putting in more miles, longer workouts, and higher intensity in one or two of the three sports. The temptation is to push, push, push, as if rest were a sin. Rest simply means ''go easy for a while.'' A 15-mile run or a two-mile swim can be leisurely, giving the body a chance to recuperate from the hard triple workout the day before.

Relentless overstressing will almost certainly result in lower performance, illness, or serious injury.

A triathlete can use the diversity of the triple-event sport to create rest opportunities without much letup in the work load. Remember Commandment No. 6 (Specificity): swimming is a rest for the legs; biking is a free ride for the swimming muscles. Even running and biking, though using many of the same leg muscles, are different enough for each to serve as a resting activity for the other.

Signs of Distress

Your body will cry out when it is in trouble. Pay attention to the following distress signals:

PAIN: Athletes can get hooked on pain if they think it means gain, and they will ignore it until it is overwhelming. In training, sharp pain means *stop immediately.* Little injuries, when heeded, can heal overnight. But permanent handicaps can develop from chronic problems.

TIREDNESS: Many different factors can cause low energy: bad diet, overtraining, stress, etc. Lethargy is a sure sign of problems.

ILLNESS: Intense exercise can decrease the body's defenses against bacteria or virus invasions. Regular submaximal exercise, on the other hand, will stimulate the body's immune system and improve its capacity to resist illness.

SLEEP: In 1966 Dr. Fred Baekland of the State University of New York demonstrated scientifically for the first time that hard physical exercise promotes deep sleep. If you're not sleeping well, something is wrong.

IRRITABILITY: Nervous tension, impatience, and bad temper are psychological indicators of physiological ill health.

OTHER SIGNS: Changes in appetite, headaches, constipation, loss of interest in training, weight changes, swelling of the lymph nodes, and absence of menstruation are often indicative of body stress. Be attentive.

Signs of Well-Being

Your body also signals its well-being. Happiness is yours when you experience the following symptoms:

JOY IN TRAINING: Exercise improves your mood. Researchers have shown that exercise is more relaxing than tranquilizers because it increases levels of norepinephrine, a natural narcotic in the brain required for transmission of messages to certain nerves. Happy people have higher levels of this hormone than those who are depressed.

FEELING OF ACCOMPLISHMENT: As you progress down the road to triple fitness your success will produce more success. (But don't strain an arm muscle as you reach around to pat yourself on the back.)

CREATIVITY: Scientists cannot explain why athletes report that they often feel very creative during training. Psychologists claim that exercise can air out the mind, allowing it to work through obstacles by turning its attention to other matters for a while.

EXERCISE FITS IN: There will always be times when staying on the crosstraining program is a struggle. When you are doing well, however, the training fits into your lifestyle and strengthens your identity. It becomes second nature. Then you know you are on the right track. Life simply becomes easier.

After you listen to your body, record its comments in your training log. Pain is usually a quick distress signal; well-being is usually a slow pleasure sign. It is best to keep track of both of them. Go back every few days, weeks, or months and reread what you have written. If you notice that you comment negatively about your training three days a week, then it is time to make an adjustment. Write not only of miles and meters but also of pain and joy.

COMMON INJURIES FOR TRIATHLETES

Many triathletes complain about triathlete knee. The knee is the most infamous joint in sports because it is subject to great abuse. Its construction as both a hinge joint and a lever joint requires that it be both mobile and stable. These are contradictory demands. The triathlete knee syndrome is caused by the contrasting action on the knee of the two leg-propelled sports. When the triathlete cycles, the knee joint is pulled apart and stretched. When the triathlete runs, the knee joint is slammed together and tightened. The opposing actions can be wrenching. Swimming does not seem to hurt the knees and may even be therapeutic.

The knee is traumatized when you run because with each leg impact your knee must support the entire weight of your body. While the force of running is cushioned by shock-absorbing soles and by foot flexion, some of the force is passed up to the knee area. Medical scientists report that runner's knee is the result of multiple tears of the bands of connective tissue around the joint. The pain is generally directed toward the outer part of the knee unless your footplant varies from the normal. Cycle-related knee problems may be due to poor pedaling technique when using toe clips. If your feet are jammed forward against the ends of the clips, not only can knee soreness develop, but much of your leg power is wasted.

Most sports physicians recommend using ice for 20 minutes twice daily for one week. This should ease the tenderness. Take two buffered aspirin tablets with each meal for several days. The aspirin will ease the inflammation. Stop running for at least one week. This gives the microtears time to heal. After a week you may start running again, but run only half the daily distance you ran prior to incurring a knee injury. If you can run pain-free for three weeks, you can return to full distances.

The standard affliction of the freestyler is swimmer's shoulder, a special type of tendinitis in the shoulder joint caused by overuse. The inflammation of the tendons will cause pain on the top of your shoulder when you raise your arm above shoulder level. Although hand paddles are great aids for resistance training, using them will cause the joint more pain if you have a slight injury. The best treatment is rest, ice therapy, and aspirin or other oral anti-inflammatory agents.

The standard afflictions of the cyclist result from collisions at high speeds with moving or stationary objects. Otherwise the sport is relatively free from the sort of injuries caused by pounding the pavement or pushing the water. The most common and irritating pain is saddle soreness caused by the heat and perspiration of exercise and the pressure of your weight. It's important, of course, to buy a well-made and well-fitting saddle; but the only real cure is more time in the saddle, so that calluses have time to develop, or rest and relaxation. Most other bicycle pains can be helped by properly adjusting the bicycle to fit your body frame.

The sport of running, unfortunately, is not blessed with the buoyancy of swimming or the smooth, steady momentum of cycling. It is, therefore, the triathlete's major cause of injury and physical pain. Look at this partial list of potential injuries: *Bursitis, tendinitis, muscle pulls, sprains, strains, soreness, tissue tears, stress fractures, joint subluxation and dislocation, patella chrondromalacia (kneecap wear and tear), shin splints, tendon rupture, plantar fasciitis, foot arch problems, bunions, bunionette, blisters, black toes.*

It's a good idea to check a specific resource book such as Southmayd and Hoffman's *Sports Health: The Complete Book of Athletic Injuries* (Music Sales Corp., New York, 1981) to study your aches and pains. Another source of information is Mirken & Hoffman's, *The Sports Medicine Book* (Little, Brown and Co., Boston, 1978).

TREATMENT OF INJURIES

The best treatment is prevention. The best means of prevention is to follow a carefully designed training program, to warm up properly, stretch, and rest between hard workouts. Unfortunately, there are biomechanical conditions which, regardless of your attention to detail, can result in a breakdown. The more quickly you can respond to an ache, pain, sprain, strain, or pull, the better your chances are for early recovery. The longer you continue with an injury or chronic condition, the more difficult it is for the body to repair itself.

The home treatment plan consists of a four-step first-aid program called *RICE:* rest, ice, compression, and elevation. Rest the injured part by keeping it immobile. Apply ice treatment frequently. Use some type of compression, such as an elastic bandage to limit swelling. Elevate the affected body part, if possible. RICE treatment should last at least 48 hours. Start heat treatments after that two-day period or after swelling is reduced.

There may be times when the injury deserves a doctor's diagnosis. Try to make an appointment with a sports medicine physician, one who specializes in treating athletes. There are no set guidelines on when to seek out a doctor's advice. Be conservative. It's best to rely on your intuition.

Rehabilitation after an injury is a must. Usually this should begin after the swelling stops. Quick rehabilitation can decrease downtime by at least 25 percent. In organized amateur and professional sports, therapists or trainers start working on an injury within 48 hours, as this decreases the atrophy and stimulates recovery. Some of the techniques they employ are ultrasound hydrocollators, short-wave diathermy, range-of-motion exercises, and transcutaneous electrical nerve stimulation.

Your goal is to minimize downtime. After all, the longer your name is on the injured list, the less time you have to develop to your peak performance. You will not be able to continue on your schedule to become fitter or faster. Time off will be a setback to your training regime.

The high cost of injury can be a financial as well as an athletic setback. Add together what you could possibly invest in doctors' visits, hospital time, and rehabilitation expenses. Add to that figure what your time is worth. Add also the possible cost of long-term damage. A joint can be strained only so many times until some permanent damage results. Your weakness can become a handicap. Your goal, then, is to maximize your uptime by heeding the warning signs, treating injuries immediately, and avoiding overtraining.

ENVIRONMENTAL CONDITIONS

Many triathlons are held under conditions well outside the comfort zone: muggy heat, blistering wind, pelting rain, rarefied elevation. It is to your advantage to train in conditions similar to those of the race. At Hawaii's International Triathlon the heat and humidity take their toll on the athletes. You need to acclimate for at least two weeks to teach your body's thermoregulatory system to respond.

Training yourself to increase liquid intake is a must. (Never take salt tablets.) When you are exercising, cold drinks are absorbed by the system faster than liquids of warmer temperature. Contrary to common thought, they do not cause stomach cramps for most people. It is better to drink small amounts of fluids frequently than to gulp larger amounts at one time. Dress appropriately for the heat—wear minimal clothing, but protect yourself from the sun.

Performances usually are below par when events are held in hot weather. The heart must work harder, your muscles do not function as efficiently, and your caloric requirement is higher. When conditions are hot *and* humid, such as in Hawaii, performance is further retarded because sweat simply does not evaporate as quickly, and your body's cooling is slowed even further. (When the weather is both hot and humid, cotton clothing is a good choice because it wicks moisture away from your body, thus aiding in lowering your body temperature.) High performance in hot, humid weather requires a higher level of adaptation and fitness.

Training in the cold is a matter of dressing correctly. Regardless of the air temperature, your body will produce heat and sweat when you exercise strenuously. If you stop exercising, the sweat will chill you rather than evaporating, and you will feel cold. Dress in layers of clothing, which you can peel off or put on as required. A T-shirt may be enough for the intense portions of a workout when you are putting out a lot of heat and perspiration; a wool jersey may be required when you slow the pace; a windbreaking shell may be sensible for times when you have to stop or sprint. Your hands, feet, and head are places where you first feel cold. If you cover them well, your core temperature can remain high. As with heat, the body acclimates to the cold. Its response is to increase the blood supply to the limbs. You are more susceptible to the effects of cold when dehydrated, after drinking alcohol, or when fatigued, injured, or poorly nourished.

HAZARDS

Swimming

When swimming in a pool, you invite illness by immersing yourself in water that may not be treated correctly. Look at the wall of the pool at water level and see if there is a ring. This is a telltale sign. Cloudy water doesn't necessarily mean that the pool is dirty or unsafe; the effect might be from a temporary chemical imbalance. Unfortunately, the chemicals used to reduce bacterial growth can also affect you. Some people are allergic to chlorine. Be aware of skin problems or other signs of irritation.

If you can, swim in open water frequently. For long lake or ocean swims, be sure you're accompanied by a paddleboard, rowboat, or motorboat for safety. Stay out of the water during thunderstorms and strong winds and watch out for sailboat and powercraft traffic. Always wear a fluorescent orange cap for visibility to boats.

Bicycling

The hazards encountered while bicycling are the most serious, because you are traveling on a rapidly moving machine over an unpredictable surface, surrounded by massive cars coming at you from all directions. The value of wearing a helmet at all times would seem obvious, yet one well-known triathlete recently took a serious spill without a helmet. The result: 57 stitches in his head. Remember, striking your unprotected head on pavement or a hard object at as slow a speed as five miles per hour can kill you.

Proper adjustment of your bicycle is crucial to both riding safety and efficiency. Take the time to adjust your bicycle properly. (See Chapter 13.) The price you pay for a loose handlebar stem, for example, is loss of control and possibly a serious injury.

Proper road safety is not only life-saving, it is the law. Ride with the traffic flow, about four feet from the right curb or row of parked cars. This affords you room to maneuver away from potholes, cars that drive too close, glass, and other road hazards. On heavily traveled streets, stay as close to the right as possible; better still, find a less crowded riding course.

At night, make yourself visible to your enemy—the car. Lights work best; reflective clothing and tape on your helmet help. Even these might not defend you against the drunken motorist, who causes more than 50 percent of all nighttime collisions with cyclists. It's best not to ride at night at all.

Always signal with your hand when making a turn. Be predictable. If you have to, shout. Look for sight contact with drivers to make sure they acknowledge your presence. Anticipate road hazards such as potholes, speed bumps, railroad or streetcar tracks, cobblestones, wet roads, wet spots, road gratings, bridges, tunnels, air blasts from large trucks and vehicles, large side mirrors, opening car doors, bugs, cars throwing dirt or exhaust into your eyes, dogs, pedestrians, and runners.

Sooner or later your number will come up and you'll take a spill. There is a right way to fall. With the grace of a true athlete, relax in the midst of disaster and don't panic. If you fall on your side and slide, go with it easily. Tuck your arms against your chest and protect your face with your hands. If you try to break the fall by putting your hands out, you will probably sprain a wrist or break an arm. Rather than suffering a few bruises, you may end up in the hospital.

Head-on collisions can result in massive damage. Try, if you can, to turn the collision into a glancing blow. Make a quick turn, first toward the car to start your body in the opposite direction and then immediately away from the car. This is a tough maneuver that requires practice, but it could save your life. If you are hit from the rear, don't brake. Accelerate instead and pull over to the right. If direct impact is inevitable, you can dump your bike and sail over the vehicle (this doesn't work well with a bus) or throw yourself away from the vehicle to the ground.

You may have a tire blow out. If you lose the front tire, you also lose steering control. Relax, don't panic. Pump your brakes until you stop. The same goes for the rear tire. If you hit the rear brakes only, you can skid; if you hit the front brakes only, you can become airborne over the handlebars. Pump both brakes.

Another form of protection is insurance. If you either own an expensive bike or crash a lot, buy an insurance policy. They run about $10 for every $100 in bike value, and most have deductible clauses. Your home policy usually covers only theft losses, not collision damage.

Don't let these hazards dismay you. Cycling is rewarding, and being prepared for dangers lessens the risk. Statistically, the accident rate in the bathroom is higher, and we all continue to take showers.

Running

Runners must also follow the rules of the road. They should run against traffic rather than with it. The same hazards that can befall a bicyclist can trip up a runner. The dogs, the hailstorms, and the cars are all part of the challenge of successfully negotiating a good workout. Since the only equipment used by the runner are shoes and clothes, just be sure that you have the best.

The most important piece of equipment for the runner is a shoe designed specifically for running, not for basketball or tennis. Think of the job the running shoe must do. Each foot strikes the ground

800 times per mile, on the average. In a five-mile run that's 4,000 contacts and, for a 140-pound person, 56,000 pounds of impact. Imagine the protection that a shoe must afford and then buy the one that fits and protects the best. Most running shoes no longer need a breaking in period.

When you buy shoes, it is helpful to consult shoe surveys in running magazines. But the most important factor is to pay close attention to how a shoe feels when you try it on and to the manufacturers' recommendations. A running shoe should fit your foot like a glove fits a hand—it should wrap all around your foot. In addition, it might be helpful to know before you buy a pair of running shoes whether you have any biomechanical abnormalities in your running style. This can spare you from injuries and perhaps save money as well. For example, a friend of mine recently found out that his right foot pronates (rolls inward excessively). Had he known that a month earlier, he wouldn't have spent $50 on a pair of training flats that, according to the manufacturer, are "not recommended for runners who pronate," and that now have a deformed heel cup on the right shoe. Also, wear bright, easily visible clothing that can be seen at night by strollers, cyclists, and cars, as well as by other runners.

Once you have purchased footwear and clothing and are ready for the run, you need only your wits. Be aware of environmental conditions such as heat, cold, humidity, rain, lightning, snow, hail, ice, wind, high altitudes, rough terrain, hills, mud, slush, fog, darkness, automobiles, dogs, and desperados. "Only the swift run lightly; only the smart continue to run."

Summary

For the triathlete, it becomes a matter of survival of the fit. Fitness indeed has its risks, but the benefits of fitness far outweigh the cost. Training and preventive maintenance lead the body toward fitness and successful competition and to health, happiness, and longevity as well. What greater combination—fitness and health—could the triple-sports specialist ask for?

13

tools of the triathlon trade

"If you make the right choice and select a properly sized, efficient machine, you'll congratulate yourself every time you get out and ride."—Tom Petrie, *City Sports Magazine,* June 1982

Triathlons synthesize three sports. If you want to maximize performance and minimize risk of injury, choosing equipment for each event is as important as training. In selecting equipment, consider what is needed to participate safely and successfully in each. As in other sports, there are fanatics who will swim only in a certain suit fabric, or pedal only a specific alloy crank wheel, or run only in a shoe with a swoosh. At the other extreme is the person who disregards the value of the right equipment, believing that fitness is everything and that the tools of the trade are of little importance.

I knew little about equipment on my first triathlon, a short one in Davis. In the run, my specialty, I strode off in high-fashion racing gear. Winning the footrace, I hopped helmetless onto my 10-speed clunker and began pedaling furiously. I soon heard *that sound.* It hits you right over the left shoulder, the whoosh as a hot cyclist on a fine machine passes you, moving with such smooth quickness that hardly more than the air flow is audible. At the lake I dismounted from the painful plastic seat and stripped to my Speedo, returned to service after college days 15 years prior. Gingerly entering the water, I immediately started to chill. No goggles, no swim cap, no experience. After one lap of a double-loop course I edged my blue frame (my body, not my bicycle) to the side of the lake and spent an hour shivering and vowing, "As soon as I get warm I'll swim that last lap." I never kept that vow. The cold sucked out my will.

Choosing equipment is difficult because of the large number of manufacturers, the controversies about what is most suitable, the wide range of costs, the constant changes in design, and the individual needs of the triathlete. It is probably best to look at each of the sports, make a grocery list, decide on your budget and needs, and slowly accumulate the tools of the triathlon trade.

SWIMMING

Ideally, swim training should take place in a pool for interval work and in a lake or ocean for cold, rough-water distance experience. You probably won't move to Malibu or dig a hole in your backyard just for triathlon training. Swimming space is available for rent at much less cost. Pools, along with their showers and locker rooms, vary in quality. Spend the time to shop for a good one. When trying to find water, look first for the long-course, 50-meter competition pools commonly found at West Coast universities, junior colleges, and private clubs. This is the only true Olympic-size pool, despite what some advertisements say. In a 50-meter pool you get used to swimming long stretches of water without turns. If you cannot find a suitable one, look for a 25-yard pool, the regulation short-course length. They are available at most YMCAs, swim clubs, public recreation areas, park departments, and high schools. As a last choice, consider the smaller pools found in health spas, motels, and backyards, though they really are unsatisfactory for a swimmer of triathlon ability.

Variables to compare when deciding on the pool:
- cost of membership or admittance

- width of lap lanes
- use of lane dividers
- proximity to work or home
- shape of the pool (avoid the kidney-shaped ones)
- indoor or outdoor facilities
- times available to individuals for lap swims
- times set aside for Masters swim groups
- cleanliness
- traffic (always remember to circle counterclockwise within a crowded lane)
- water temperature (preferably 78–84° F.)
- the frills: weight room, whirlpool, sauna, etc.

You may prefer to work out solo during the least crowded periods of recreational lap-swim hours, or you may want an organized workout with other swimmers and a timing clock. Either way, consider buying an instructor's time for invaluable advice on stroke mechanics. Find somebody who knows how to identify your problems and communicate corrections effectively.

These days, swimming in the nude is a sensual delight reserved for dolphins. People must wear swimsuits. At least modern designs and materials reduce the effect of their presence, even visually. Men's suits barely make concessions to modesty, and women's apparel is becoming more daring. Controversy currently is raging about the two-piece suit connected down the back with a slim strap so that it can qualify as a one-piece, which the rules require. This almost-bikini is still outlawed from competition. However, with test results clearly showing that the suit produces faster swimming times, the rule probably will change. Swimming might become the first timed sport in which women perform on a par with men—if the handicap of modesty is ever stripped away.

When buying a suit, try it on and practice a dry-land version of the freestyle and the frog kick to see if it fits comfortably on moving muscles. It should not slip or rub. Manufacturers today produce racing suits made of either nylon (more durable, less expensive— usually used as workout suits) or Lycra/spandex (better fit and

Goggles, cap, and swim suit are the basics but add hand-paddles as a helpful training device.

comfort—competitive suits with good strength and durability). These Lycra/spandex skin suits, available to both men (cost: $10–20) and women (cost: $15–40), are sleek, taut, and featherlight. Rinse them in fresh water after each use, handwash with soap every fourth wearing, and let them drip dry.

State-of-the-art swim goggles have yet to be designed. Current models leak, fog, and are uncomfortable. They do protect your eyes from irritation caused by water-borne chemicals, however, and aid your underwater vision. With goggles it's easier to see the ends of the pool, swim lanes, and other swimmers. Fit is important, and there is no other way to get a good fit other than to try on different brands at a specialty shop. Each brand seems to have a different curvature across the brow and cheek. You have a choice of lens colors: blue; green or gray (which shield your eyes from the bright sunlight); yellow or pink (to brighten the contrast of indoor lighting); and clear. To prevent leaks, adjust the rubber headband around the back of your head and the center strap over your nose. Compress the lens against your face for a more secure fit. To prevent fogging you can use spit (doesn't work well), defogging compound, or contact-lens cleaning solutions with antifogging agents. Always wipe away the excess chemicals. The life span of goggles is about a year. Cost: $3–6.

People with myopia, hyperopia, or astigmatism have two choices: either put prescription lenses into the goggles or wear contact lenses with properly fitting goggles. Manufacturers can permanently bond your prescription lenses to any make of goggles you supply. Contact Opti-Sport Co., 2460 Williamette St., Eugene, OR 97405, (503) 986-1237; or Poolmaster, 160 Jefferson Dr., Menlo Park, CA, (800) 227-8355.

Triathletes should consider purchasing open-water goggles as well as pool goggles. Open-water goggles are larger and have wider elastic bands and wider rubber to obtain a tighter seal with your face. Several types of open-water goggles are manufactured. Speedo has a model called "Ultravision," and Barracuda makes a similar goggle. For cold-water swimming, a must is Scuba Pro's "Rough Water," which is one of the few free-diving masks that is small and keeps your face warm.

Swim caps or bathing caps, as they are sometimes called, keep your hair dry and your head warm. There are two types: rubber caps, which cost about $2–4 and the newer Lycra ones, which cost $3–7. Try to air dry them between swims. Some people dust talcum powder on them to keep the sides from sticking together. Triathletes with long hair will find that swim caps reduce hair-drying time.

Training Devices

At sport shops or membership pools you can buy devices designed to improve your stroke mechanics or to create greater resistance in the water, thereby increasing the work load on the muscles. While these extras can help increase the effectiveness of your swimming workouts, none of them are absolutely necessary. Some of these devices include the following:

KICKBOARDS: These rectangular slabs of hard foam, used to work on either the kick or the arm pull, cost $4–8.

SWIM FINS: Used by competitive swimmers to add variety to workouts, develop leg strength, and place an overload on the cardiovascular system, swim fins can be purchased for $10 or more.

PULLBUOYS: Styrofoam twin cylinders connected with a cord or strap, used to support your legs so that you can work on upper body strength and technique and add variety to your workout, can be bought for $4–6.

HAND PADDLES: These plastic plates fit on your hand and work to strengthen your shoulders, chest, back, and arms in the same way that fins work on the lower body—increasing resistance and overloading the muscles. A must for the serious triathlete, they cost $4–7.

DONUTS: These round rubber rings are twisted around the ankles and work like pullbuoys. They cost $5–10.

OTHER DEVICES: Other mechanical devices that you can use to improve your swimming resistance are drag suits (vests with pockets that catch water and slow you down), extra layers of swimsuits, T-shirts, kickboards with scooped-out bottoms, and weights around your wrists and ankles.

BICYCLING

When the time comes for bicycle selection and fit, clamp down hard on the brakes and give the matter careful consideration. There is much to know, and the details are sometimes confusing. To the aficionado cyclist, all is simple and clear: the finest alloy wheels attached to an ultralight frame and the words Campagnolo stamped on all the other components. To people used to less complicated sports, the jargon of cycling suggests that there is a lot of mechanical bother. Not only do you have to buy an expensive thoroughbred machine, but you have to custom-design it, fix it, adjust it, understand it, conform to it, power it, and babysit it. This is only partly true.

Your first best buy is a good bicycling book such as John Marino's *Bicycling Book* (J. P. Tarcher, Inc., Los Angeles, 1981) or Tom Lieb's *Everybody's Book of Bicycle Riding* (Rodale Press, Inc., Emmaus, PA, 1981). *Bicycling* magazine is also an excellent source. (See, for example, the February 1983 issue. It has an excellent article on how to select a bicycle and a comparison of the major brands and models.) After you've read up on the subject, go shopping at a specialty bicycle shop. Be armed with some information. Tell them your situation and your budget and ask for some suggestions.

There are a few considerations of particular interest to triathletes who are new to the bike scene. Basically, there are two parts to bicycles: the frame and the components. When you purchase a stock bike, you take these together unless your shop will agree to trade-ins on stock components. The standard recreational 10-speed is made of straight-gauge, high-carbon steel tubing, while the top-of-the-line 10-speed frames are constructed of double-butted chrome-molybdenum alloy steel tubing and silver solder. Custom frames range in price from $400 to $1,000. The components (everything except the frame) include wheels, tires, derailleurs, crankset, handlebars, brakes, seat. You are going to have to decide between sew-up tires and high-pressure clinchers, between center pull and side pull brakes, and whether or not to pay for expensive but lightweight alloy construction in the components.

You have two frame design choices: touring or road racing. Both are acceptable for triathlon competition. The racing bike has a shorter wheelbase, to maximize pedal power. The longer tourer is more flexible and therefore more comfortably shock-absorbing. Triathletes who are proficient cyclists aiming for world-class performance will choose the road-racing bike. Triathletes who won't be leading the pack and want to get the most out of their

Ardis Bow finished the 1982 IRONMAN in sixth place on her ill-fitting Bianchi. Notice her elbows and knees in contact and the poor angles at ankles and hips.

investment recreationally will be happiest with a touring bike. Select the size frame that fits your body dimensions. Stock bikes should at least be fit to leg length; custom frames can be built proportionately to fit the upper body.

Gearing differs between the road racer and the tourer. Typical racing bikes have front chain wheels with 53 and 42 teeth, rear cogs of 13–28 teeth. Typical touring bikes have front chain wheels of 52 and 36 teeth, rear cogs of 14–34 teeth. In both you will find the high gear combinations necessary for good speed on level roads or downhill. The touring bike has alpine gears made for pulling grades with heavy loads. The racing bike's low gear range demands greater leg strength while going up steep hills. (See Chapter 10 for more information on gearing.)

It takes about an hour to adjust the bicycle to your body size. Spend it. The joys of riding comfortably and efficiently depend on this proper fit. The bicycle, after all, is a machine that has been designed around you, the human engine. If the bicycle is compatibly matched to you, the energy expended in pedaling is efficiently converted into forward motion—the direction to the finish line.

What you have to decide when you buy a bicycle is what you want to do with it, both in triathlons and apart from them. Some people look for the best buy, and some people have to buy the best. Bicycles certainly give you the chance to direct yourself toward either extreme. My advice is to decide what role the bicycle plays in your life and then buy the best one you can afford to buy to suit that purpose. A range of possibilities are described on the next pages followed by a list of useful accessories.

There has been a lot of improvement in bike technology in the past 10 years. You can get a much better bike for the same dollar value now than you could a decade ago, particularly where components are concerned. Ten years ago, if you wanted a good bike, you bought a top-of-the-line Raleigh or Peugeot for $250–300, and the quality of the components was decent. But if you bought a bike one or two notches down, the brazing and paint were likely to be less than perfect, and the quality of the components was generally crude. By comparison, the Univega or Fuji you can buy today (yes, it's the Japanese who have made the real progress in this industry, too) would make the bicycle of 10 years ago look unrefined. For $300–600 you can get a bicycle with a high-quality frame and elegant, smooth-functioning, durable alloy components. In 1983 dollars it's hard to get a good new bike with desirable features for high performance (alloy rims and hubs, quality derailleurs and pedals, high-pressure tires, light weight, quick-release hubs, cotterless alloy crank) for less than $300.

By the way, probably the most important single components that make a difference in performance are the *wheels.* Spend a little extra money to get good-quality alloy hubs and light, strong alloy rims. Have the hubs adjusted properly. These steps will significantly reduce rolling resistance, as will the purchase of high-pressure tires. (For a more complete discussion of tire and rim selection, see Chapter 10, The Fine-Tuned Triathlete.)

Of course, you can spend more if you want to. You can get a handmade custom frame of double-butted Reynolds 531 or Columbus tubing dressed out with Campagnolo Super Record components, heat-treated Ambrosio rims and silk sew-ups, and shell out $2,000 for it. You can if you want to, but you don't need to.

By the way, since bicycles are relatively simple machines, it's not a bad idea to consider a good-quality used bike. Hang out in enthusiast bike shops and sniff around—listen to the regulars and check out the bulletin boards. "Bikies" are always looking to trade up, just like sports car nuts. You can get a good used bike for 50 to 75 percent of what a new one would cost. And if you don't know bikes really well, find somebody who does that you can trust to help you pick one out.

Accessories

Let's assume you have your bike. There are some bicycle accessories/components that are really useful. They make riding more efficient and/or enjoyable. They are listed in approximate order of importance.

TOE CLIPS—Toe clips are essential. They hold your feet in the right position on the pedals and allow you to nearly double your pedaling efficiency, since you can pull the pedal up as well as push it down. It takes a little while to get used to them, but in short order you can intuitively guide your foot into the clip. They come in small, medium, and large sizes.

FOAM HANDLEBAR GRIPS—These go by various brand names, but they've all made handlebar tape obsolete. Inexpensive, durable, easy to install, this kind of grip will really save your hands and shoulders in an ultratriathlon.

PUMP—Get a good pump to clip to the frame. Silca and Zefal are

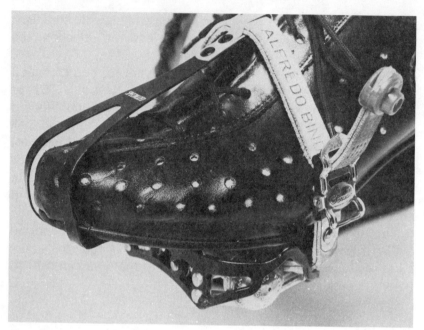

For efficient peddle power, toe clips are mandatory.

the best-known brands. Your clincher tubes should have Presta valves; they're easier to fill to high pressure and have a better seal. Sew-ups all come with Presta valves. Mount on the head tube.

WATER BOTTLES—Get two or three. You can mount them on the seat tube, on the downtube, and on a holder in front of the head tube. Get them with easy-open spouts so you can drink on the ride.

TIRE SAVERS—These are little plastic-covered wires that scrape dirt off your tires and (supposedly) help prevent blowouts—cheap insurance for about $1.50.

QUICK-RELEASE SEAT POST SKEWER—Hardly a necessity, and not always easy to find, but this component allows you to change the adjustment on your seat or remove it easily. It works just like the ones on your wheels.

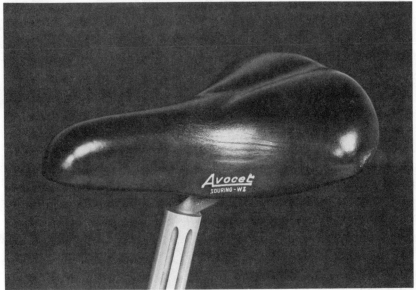

Comfort starts here—get the best you can afford. Try out various makes just as you would different shoes.

CYCLOCOMPUTER—This is an interesting gadget as well as a useful training tool. For $60–100 you can get a lightweight, convenient electronic monitor that will give you current, average, and maximum speeds, elapsed time and distance, and will serve as a trip meter.

There are also some important personal accessories that you wear or that come in close contact with your body.

SADDLE—Get the best you can afford. You wouldn't buy shoes that don't fit your feet, so don't buy a saddle that doesn't conform to your ischial tuberosities (pelvic protrusions). Brooks and Ideale are old-line manufacturers; Avocet makes a line of touring and racing saddles designed for men and women; and Concor, from Italy, is popular with heavy riders. See if you can try out a friend's saddle or if your dealer can accommodate some experimentation on your part. You'll really curse yourself if you don't take enough time with saddle selection; you'll be in absolute misery even in a short triathlon.

HELMET—If you want to use your head for good sense instead of bouncing on the pavement, a helmet is the best $40–50 invest-ment you will ever make. People who don't wear helmets (real bike helmets, not leather racing helmets) are fools. A helmet can save your brains, even your life. Always wear one. Buy one designed for the sport. They are made by Bell, Protec, MSR, and Skid-lid.

SUNGLASSES, REARVIEW MIRROR—A good pair of wraparound sunglasses will protect your eyes from the rays of the sun, the wind, and flying objects. You can get a little clip-on mirror for your glasses or helmet that makes it really convenient (and safer) to check traffic conditions behind you.

GLOVES—Even if you have padded handlebars, a good set of padded gloves will save your hands from getting numb from road shock on long rides and scraped up should you fall. They also keep sweaty hands from slipping on the bars.

SHOES—A good pair of riding shoes is an important investment— you'll be spending as much time in them as on your bike. There are racing and touring shoes. The racing shoes feature an inner metal shank for protection and as a base to pedal on. The lighter the shoe, the better (most weigh 1½–2 pounds) because you have to lift that foot with each revolution, and ounces add up. Properly fitting your cleats to the pedal is important.

SHORTS—In the apparel line, riding shorts are made of stretchy fabric sewn together with smooth seams and lined with chamois skin in the crotch area. The material is either wool (which is warmer and wick dries) or synthetic (machine washable), cut longer in the thigh to prevent chafing with the seat, low in the front for ease of breathing, and high in the back to cover you as you lean forward. They are worn without underwear. A pair of bike shorts is an invaluable asset on long rides.

JERSEY—The bicycle jersey is designed for comfort, safety, and convenience. It is made of a variety of materials—wool for cool weather, cotton-polyester for hot climates, or Spandex-nylon, called *second skin*. Jerseys feature bright colors so automobile drivers can see you and a wide pocket along the back to store a tire patch kit or fruit for lunch. T-shirts work well in hot weather if they are long in the back. All upper- and lower-body apparel should fit snugly to prevent excess wind drag.

Cold-weather cycling presents added apparel requirements. Look for good ventilation under extreme conditions combined with good windbreaking characteristics. Ski gloves are well suited for protection from cold wind. Protect your leather saddle in the rain with a plastic bag. A knit ski hat will fit under your helmet for warmth (in really cold weather you will need the kind with holes for your eyes, nose, and mouth). Leg warmers, polypropylene long johns, or long cycling pants are important for protecting the knees, which break the wind and have little blood circulation. Remember that on your cycle the temperature is 20–30 degrees colder than the outside air due to the wind-chill factor.

You are now athletically set up, and financially set back. An alternative is either to buy a used bicycle or to buy a bike with a good basic frame to which you can gradually add better components. This spreads the payment plan out longer, though at a higher cost because the markup is greater on piecemeal sales.

Adjusting the Bike to Fit

In order to ride efficiently and comfortably, you need to adapt your bicycle to your own needs. The bicycle–human body relationship is determined by certain considerations, such as frame size and adjustment of the bicycle's component parts. Here are some basic guidelines to follow to adjust your bicycle to its human engine.

FRAME SIZE—Bicycle frame sizes usually come in 19, 21, 23, and 25 inches, or the metric equivalents thereof. This represents the distance between the top of the seat tube and the middle of the

Saddle height angle adjustment.

bottom bracket. To find out if a bike frame fits you, straddle it. With your feet about a foot apart from each other, there should be about two or three inches between your actual crotch (not just the crotch of your pants) and the top tube. You may need to vary this distance if you have very long legs and a short trunk or the reverse. Since frame geometry remains constant, if you have long legs and a short torso, you may wish to choose a shorter frame. Otherwise you will find yourself stretched out uncomfortably over the top tube (since a bike with a longer seat tube has a longer top tube). So you may have to make up for having a relatively long or short torso in the seat adjustment.

SADDLE—It is very important to have the saddle in the correct position. There are three adjustments to consider: angle, height, and forward or backward position. As far as *angle* is concerned, the saddle should be level or have the front tipped up slightly. Use a measuring stick (see photo) to determine this.

On the left, the saddle is too high; on the right, the height has been correctly adjusted.

This is the best method to find the "neutral" position for the saddle.

Next, adjust for saddle height. Ask a friend to hold the bike while you sit on it barefoot, with your heels on the pedals. Choose a saddle height that you think is too low and pedal backward. Raise the saddle until your hips slide up and down as you complete a revolution of the crank (see photo). Once this sliding from side to side takes place, lower the seat post about ½ inch.

To find the neutral (backward-forward) position for the saddle, find the saddle position in which a plumb line intersects both the bone beneath and to the outside of the kneecap and the pedal axle (with the pedals horizontal). This is shown in the photo; adjust the saddle forward or backward to this point.

PEDALS—For every 2,000 miles that a cyclist rides, he rotates the pedals about a million times. Make sure that the ball of your foot sits over the pedal axle. This can best be accomplished through the use of toe clips, which you should buy in the appropriate size (S-M-L). Point your foot straight ahead, not toed in or toed out. Keep ½ inch between the front of your shoe and the front of the toe clip. This will allow you to deliver power to the crank throughout the entire revolution.

STEM HEIGHT AND LENGTH—The stem height should be one or two inches below the height of the saddle (see the first photo in this series again). The length of the stem should be such that the cyclist in the ideal riding position sees the front hub in a direct line with the end of the stem.

HANDLEBARS—The width you choose for handlebars depends on the width of your shoulders and can be 38, 40, or 42 cm. Select the width that best corresponds to your shoulder width. Position the handlebars so that from a side view, the tops of the bars are parallel to the top tube.

RUNNING GEAR

How simple this sport is! There are no elaborate facilities, and there is no machinery to break down—just clothing, which should

The bare essentials for running apparel.

cost you less than $100 altogether. You'll get top-of-the-line training shoes that provide good heel stability, toe room, shock absorption capacity, flexibility, soles that you like, and comfort. Manufacturers now produce more than 400 styles and colors for you to choose from, and it will require about 30 minutes in a running-apparel store to pick out the right ones. Trust your feet, not the sales pitch; they know best. *Take your time.* A hasty choice will make your feet suffer. Manufacturers have specialized to the point that you will probably be able to find a shoe designed for the kind of runner you are. If you're heavy, have narrow or wide feet, are hard on shoes, want lots of rear foot support, need plenty of cushion, or run mostly on trails, don't despair. There's a running shoe out there for you.

Other pieces of clothing include high-bulk orlon socks, tricot nylon shorts, a T-shirt or jersey; cold weather clothes such as long pants, rain suit, gloves, hat, or mask. That is one appealing characteristic of running. You don't need a lot of equipment, and what you need doesn't cost a lot. There are a few useful accessories you might want to consider. A wristwatch is valuable for measuring your workouts, and reflective tape or a reflective vest helps you to be seen by cars if you run at night.

TRIATHLON SPECIALTY PRODUCTS

Specific triathlon specialty products have been created both to improve athletes' performance through functional design and to upgrade their appearance through fashion coordination. Several manufacturers have produced special triathlon activewear that allows you to don one outfit and participate in all three events without changing clothes. This saves you anywhere from 2–20 minutes in the transition period. Dave Horning left the swim portion of the February 1982 Ironman Triathlon in tenth place. Wearing a one-piece triathlon suit, he avoided the changing corrals, slipped on his cycling cleats, and started the bicycle race in second place, saving more than eight minutes and moving ahead eight places— all of this simply because of his functional and fashionable clothing.

A triathlon short made of Spandex-nylon called a *tri-skin short* has been designed to serve for all three sports. Men simply add a cycling jersey, then slip on a tricot running singlet. Women frequently wear their Speedo suit for the swim and then slip on the Tri-Skin Short for cycling and running. The short is made of Spandex-nylon with a drawstring for swimming, has shorter than cycle-length legs, and no chamois crotch. (Chamois crotches were designed for wool shorts to prevent chafing and to cushion your bottom. Put padding on your seat, not in your shorts.) The properties of Spandex-nylon eliminate chafing. They are available through Tri-Triathlon, 2410 J Street, Sacramento, CA 95816; (916) 442-8326.

Other triathlon products will be on the market in the near future. Specially designed triathlon cycling-running shoes are in the experimental stage. Workout outfits, T-shirts, tank tops, swim caps, new goggle designs, as well as accessories such as travel bags, bike caps, and after-the-race triathlon fashion will be commonplace. The sport is inviting entrepreneurs to develop ideas that will enhance the aficionado's appreciation of the multisport race.

Shop for your triathletic gear in specialty sport shops. Salespeople in discount houses, department stores, or hardware stores know little about your needs. They all sell bikes, swim gear, and footwear, but they lack the motivation and knowledge to be helpful. The people at specialty shops, however, will help pick out the right gear to meet your needs, your body size, and your budget. The running-shoe shop will have a wide selection of top-quality brands, and one of those makes will fit you as if it were custom-made. The bike shop will set up the bike properly and will respond helpfully if you have problems or need repairs. Find out from the aficionados which retail businesses are best known for their service and expertise. In a good specialty shop you will find friendly people who understand athletes, because they are frequently athletes themselves.

14

conditioning the mental muscles

"Great challenge; great race; you are beautiful, but I don't need to race you anymore. I have overcome myself so much and reached a point where I am in tune with my physical and mental abilities. I now have perfect control of what I am doing. That, to me, is the ultimate athlete."

The race starts long before the opening gun. You picture yourself at the starting line, ready to explode, to direct your incredible energy outward onto the course. A phantom starter slowly raises her hand and squeezes the trigger, the gun fires, and you're off—a videotape replay of a race that hasn't yet happened. That mental videocassette system is called *visualization*. It is one of 10 peaking principles I use to make it all come together in competition. Sports scientists seem to shy away from discussion of the psychological aspects of maximizing performance, because the phenomena are difficult to identify, measure, and analyze in clinical terms. It is easier to measure maximum oxygen uptake than max alpha waves. Nonetheless, the mind is the most important muscle, and it, too, requires conditioning.

Mark Montgomery is totally tuned in to the race.

PEAKING PRINCIPLE #1

Visualize a successful race and practice the process of previewing your game plan through the process of mental rehearsal.

When Dave Horning from Berkeley, California, finished first in the 1981 Escape from Alcatraz Triathlon, the outcome, for him, was anticlimactic. He had mentally replayed the race so often and was so familiar with the scene at the finish—Dave Horning breaking the tape—that it lacked any sense of drama. Of course, the spectators did not know that he had visualized winning and probably supposed that his lack of enthusiasm was due to fatigue. The terms *visualization, imagining,* and *mental rehearsal* can, in effect, be used interchangeably. They all refer to the process of previewing an upcoming event in your mind's eye. By vividly imagining the upcoming challenge, you become more familiar and comfortable. Since your subconscious does not distinguish between real experience and imagined experience, you can write your own script with whatever outcome you desire. Your internal television screen can then play back your successful effort, removing doubt and replacing it with positive expectations.

PEAKING PRINCIPLE #2

Develop the ability to sustain your pace or your percentage of maximum output.

Mind-body feedback is necessary to maintain high effort or to handle a heavy work load. An analogy might be the thermostat of a furnace, reading the room temperature and adjusting the output of heat accordingly. You must pay attention to and monitor the stress your body is undergoing and regulate your own "throttle." Ideally, you try to keep the intensity of the race pace even, but there are times when you can enhance your performance at only a little extra energy cost. I call this pace-sensing ability your "perceptostat."

How do you know how high you can afford to set your perceptostat in order to maximize performance? This is a difficult question to answer, and only experience will provide you with most of the clues. Through racing and crosstraining, you will get to know your body; this is a learned skill resulting from athletic maturity that only time and experience give. This is one of the few advantages that older triathletes have over younger ones—knowing pacing and its effects on the available energy you have stored.

Sometimes, of course, even when you're monitoring your body and pacing yourself well, fatigue can unexpectedly step in. Then you just have to grit your teeth, reach inside your mind, and find that pathway to your determination, no matter how narrow it may have become. You have to *focus*—get that look of determination in your eyes, the one that comes when you put your sense of being and self-worth on the line and push toward the finish.

PEAKING PRINCIPLE #3

Concentrate all your attention on the race.

Pain, breathing, fatigue, stiffness—all are sensory outputs that can be monitored by concentrating on your body's information switchboard. When running in the Western States 100-Mile Endurance Race in the summer of 1981, I felt a multitude of sensations throughout the 20 hours and 7 minutes of the race. It was as if I were in a trance that united all existence with my mantra, the steady beat of my footsteps. I was in a state of total concentration, an awareness of all conditions, people, feelings, and experiences.

Studies of top performers have considered this question: Do winners *associate* or *disassociate* during racing? That is, do they pay attention to what is going on with their bodies and the environment they find themselves in, or do they put their mind on autopilot, perhaps strap on a Walkman, slip in a tape of the Doobies, and drift off into outer space? The unqualified answer was the former; really top performers are in touch with their minds and bodies—

are in the here-and-now—almost all the time. Frank Shorter, for example, knows his body so well that he can run 10 miles without his watch and be accurate in estimating the distance he's run to within 100 yards. Champions are aware of nearly every move they make, every feeling and thought they have, especially when they are racing. They concentrate totally on their performance.

PEAKING PRINCIPLE #4

Take the summits and valleys of a race in stride and ride out the weak and strong periods.

During a race, why do we vacillate between feeling good and feeling lousy? It probably has to do with blood-sugar levels, secretions from endocrine glands, the way we remove metabolic waste products, or the effects of strenuous exertion on the nervous system. Sports scientists have work to do here. You know that you are going to experience high and low cycles many times over. Then, when the athletic high is present, you can enjoy it, and when the low appears you can endure it until it passes.

In an attempt to be the first woman to win the Lake Tahoe 72-Mile Race, I decided to experiment with some new substances. The year was 1978, and running magazines were expounding about the benefits of taking aspirin, coffee, vitamins, and minerals. During the first 50 miles of the race I tried them all. (There is a lesson here: never experiment in a race. Do your experimenting in training.) At the 50-mile point my gastrointestinal tract rebelled with such sharp, striking pains that I was ready to toss in the towel and call it quits. It was one of the lowest periods I'd ever experienced in a race. Fortunately, a Shiatsu therapist came along and treated me with his magic hands. He simply depressed a spot near my navel, and my stomach felt as if a watermelon had burst inside it. Everything that had been plugging me up seemed to flow into my intestinal tract, and I felt immediate relief. Moments later I was running well again, feeling high, on an emotional peak.

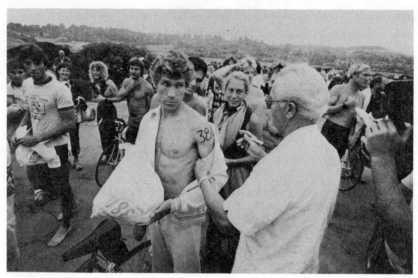

Don't allow the rat of doubt to nibble away at your resolve.

PEAKING PRINCIPLE #5

Consult yourself; you are your own coach.

You've heard the cries of some coaches as their athletes round the track. They shout, "Go for it," or "Pick up the pace." How do they know what you need or how you feel? You are your own best source of information on how your performance is progressing and the best stimulus for doing better. During the 1981 Western States 100, a television interviewer asked me as I was walking up a steep incline—at a time when I was in second place—if my strategy had changed because someone else had taken the lead. I responded, "It's me against the clock. If my clock gets to the finish line before hers, then I win; if her clock gets there before mine, she wins."

Some athletes try to psych out other athletes with put-down games, surges, passing techniques. Rather, it is best to heed your own game plan, one that you the athlete and you the coach designed together.

You need to include a constant here-and-now check system in your game plan. During races I am constantly hooking up an "engine analyzer" and asking my body parts for readouts on their current status. Usually I start with my feet and work upward, checking out my internal and external body parts. I also include a check of my mental and emotional condition—my level of determination, analysis of my highs and lows, how thirsty I am, whether my stomach is upset, whether I'm hungry, how many hours I am into the race, and how much time there is left to go. I am a coach and consultant to myself in training and even more during a race.

PEAKING PRINCIPLE #6

Be ready to counter self-doubt.

The voices of doubt and defeat will be lurking along the race route, and you had better be ready with an answer. As the miles go by, what begins as a little rat's whisper grows to a thunderous shout: "Why are you doing this to yourself? You are tired of this pain. Slow down, because the race doesn't really matter." The argument becomes more and more persuasive and your mind more and more susceptible. You can rationalize slowing down because it isn't your day or you're too fat or you didn't train enough or it really isn't important after all. How can you anticipate and counter such psychological deterioration?

First, always keep in mind why you were attracted to the test in the beginning and why you kept going throughout training. Second, when you draw up your game plan, organize the race into components, subdivide the event into successive time frames or mileage markers, and concentrate on achieving those incremental goals. Do not think of the entire race as a relentless continuum.

An example of this is the way I approached the swimming portion of the principle triathlon contest. I had expected the swim to be the most difficult part; in fact, it was the easiest for me because it was the first and shortest event. Triathletes swim 1.2 miles to a boat and then back to shore. During the swim, I thought only about the swim, giving no consideration to the 112-mile bicycle race or the 26.2-mile run that followed. The only requirement that I made for myself was to swim to the boat. When I arrived there and discovered that my body was still strong and eager, I then changed the requirement to a swim back to shore. I did this throughout the entire race, and the whole 141 miles thus became a succession of finish lines, none of them so distant that the rat of doubt could nibble at my resolve.

PEAKING PRINCIPLE #7

Be intelligent; know when to quit, and quit when the price of continuing is too high.

Many athletes are unable to retire from the race; they simply won't quit no matter how severe the pain or damage. Recently a 13-year-old friend of mine entered his first marathon. I was on the sideline as he approached the 20-mile marker, and I saw him walking in excruciating pain. He insisted on finishing; after all, his 15-year-old brother was a 2:50 marathoner. At the finish line he was taken to the hospital with a broken leg bone (the head of the trochanter). He may not be able to run for the next several years—a very high price to pay for pride.

Quitting doesn't mean that you are a loser or that the little rat's voice won the argument. It can be a sign of intelligence.

There are times when you should quit. I set up criteria for that decision prior to the race, and sometimes I'm forced to keep that agreement with myself. These criteria are strictly individual. For some rather unsportsmanlike athletes, the only criterion is position. If they aren't in the lead at a certain point in the race, they quit (or, as it is so politely stated, "drop"). For others of us the challenge is the finish line, not our position among the challenged. When setting up your quitting criteria you should consider the long-term effects of continuing in the race while injured.

In the February 1982 Iron(wo)man event in Hawaii, Pat Hines, from Los Angeles, was the first woman both to exit the water and to dismount from her bicycle. Yet she knew that she was lame from a stress fracture and only hoped that that day she would be able to muster up a marathon performance. With her lead of about 30 minutes, she strode out in high gear, only to drop out of the race at mile nine. As she walked, in unmatched pain, she vowed to return to the event totally sound. Her decision was a hard one to make, but the wisest ones never come easily.

PEAKING PRINCIPLE #8

Anxiety interferes with performance, so take time to relax.

When we arrived in Hawaii for the 1981 race I saw one of my training partners, who had come to Hawaii before we had so that he could get acclimated to the conditions. He looked worn out and unkempt, with sunken eyes and a frazzled appearance. Knowing what a powerful athlete he was, I still expected a sterling performance from him, but his time was off what he was capable of by at least one hour. Why? In part because he was unable to relax. Tension only steals calories, tightens your muscles, scrambles the brain. It is not a productive part of your game plan.

Relaxing into sterling performances is an emotional talent that comes from an ability within yourself to keep the fires roaring and your mind at ease. To stay relaxed requires that you have confidence in yourself and that you are able to listen to your body and respond to its changes. If you use the here-and-now system of checks, your mind can make adjustments; it can soothe the body to perform evenly and smoothly. Practice this technique on training runs and during races. You will be amazed at the extra energy that is freed for performance.

PEAKING PRINCIPLE #9

Pain is the monkey on the athlete's back.

Tom Warren has been a confident triathlon competitor for over five years.

There are different kinds of pain. Some pain can be ignored, and some should be heeded. Some should be welcomed. You know that the race is going to hurt. You can ignore low-grade pain or stress and heed the intense pain of injury. But you thrive on the pain of maximizing your performance. This kind of pain is easily forgotten, like the pain of childbirth or the race run a year ago. Your muscles may be stiff as those of a corpse, your feet feeling like ingots, your stomach threatening rebellion, your lungs gasping for air, and your brain hoping that the finish line is within meters. Such pain is the by-product of an ultraperformance.

There are ways of reducing pain during performance, especially the low-grade type. One of these is to focus on the locus of pain, directing your mind to that location and working on some biofeedback ways of sending relief to it. Another method is to apply hand pressure to the side (as with abdominal stretches) and hold the pressure there for several minutes. Changing the angle of your swimming stroke or the gait of your running style or shifting your weight on the bike can cause relief of a specific stress. But beware; it can produce stress in another area. If your problem is with your feet, unlace your shoes, add or remove an insert, change your socks, change the pressure on the laces, or change your shoes. In all cases, do something different. If all else fails, you can follow champion swimmer Don Schollander's advice when he was asked about pain: "If you push through the pain barrier into real agony, you're a champion."

PEAKING PRINCIPLE #10

Establish your self-confident identity.

You are in large measure what you do. You are not a quitter; you are not a fool. You are the winner, the champion, the hero—whatever the outcome. You have worked for this moment for months, perhaps years, preparing for the opportunity to be a contestant. Your videotape is running hot, recording the entire scene for later assimilation, learning from the bad parts and cherishing only the good ones.

It is now time to assimilate the final peak principle of self-identity: the ability to wrap your mind around the entire experience, to make the experience a part of your second nature. Your attitude, your posture, your way of being is one of striding off with the confidence that conquers any stretch of water, any road, any path.

You are an athlete by both birth and design, by education and training, by choice and by consequence. You are the adult in charge; you are the experience you create for yourself.

15

the victors

"When asked who is the best athlete of all, I answer that it is neither the swimmer, the runner, nor the cyclist; it is indeed the triathlete who is the champion."—Scott Tinley, Ironman, February 1982

Dave Horning (Berkeley, California)
Age: 34
Winner, 1981 and 1982 Escape from Alcatraz
Winner, 1982 International Oxford Triathlon

Dave Horning stands 6'0'' and weighs (depending on the intensity of his athletic pursuits) between 175 and 210 pounds. He has a muscular, thick, swimmer's body, bright blue eyes, and an outgoing personality to complete the picture. He is one of those people with an infectious smile and an easygoing attitude.

Horning started swimming competitively at the age of six and began to run in competition in his high school cross-country program as a 170-pound sophomore. He has always been *big*. At Cal, Dave swam distance freestyle only, missing qualifying for the nationals by mere tenths of a second. Then, as he puts it, he finished the swimming season in March, "hopped out of the pool on a Sunday, and started running track on a Monday. The track coach said, 'Sure, run for a week or two and we'll give you a time trial.' That's what we did, and I ran the mile in 4:25 against myself. At the end of the week I fell flat on my face with acute Achilles tendinitis." That ended Dave's track career.

Dave Horning—winner of the 1981 and 1982 Escape from Alcatraz and the 1982 International Oxford Triathlon.

As a collegiate athlete, Dave suffered two epileptic seizures (not in competition or training) and was told that he could never compete in athletics again. He overcame this obstacle through positive thinking and a "can do" attitude that wouldn't allow any roadblocks to stand in his way. His achievements are proof that he has been successful in this endeavor.

Broken bones sustained in a skiing accident kept Dave out of the Army, but not out of sports. He decided to try marathoning and after multiple injuries, including a stress fracture, he ran his best time in 1979, a 2:46, when he weighed 198 pounds. Dave always quotes his times in conjunction with his weights. They are related, especially if you are a big man and have to move that weight a long distance.

Dave first learned of triathlons in a 1979 *Sports Illustrated* article on the Ironman competition and knew that he had to try one. His first experience in a triathlon was in October 1979 in Davis, California, a run-bike-swim sequence. He hit that 65-degree water in first place with a high body (core) temperature and cramped up, finishing the race in 2 hours, 17 minutes, in seventh place. He tried a few more triathlons and finished some; others were fraught with equipment breakdowns or problems brought on by lack of training.

The year 1981 was his year of great triathlons. He won two in northern California—the Davis Triathlon and the Escape from Alcatraz, which includes a swim in the San Francisco Bay and a Double Dipsea run with a short bike ride in between. He finished both with large leads. For the first time he had trained sufficiently. The year 1982 has been one of sterling triathlon performances. Although heat exhaustion caused his demise in Hawaii's Ironman, he returned to win the International Oxford Triathlon in Maryland and set a new course record. In his debut in the USTS (United States Triathlon Series) in Long Beach, California, Dave finished fourth in this marathon-length event.

Bicycling is not Horning's best event, but he is good—he feels that this is the hardest part of the race for him. Of course, he likes the swim best, since he knows that he can push through the water and not heed to pacing as he must with the other two sports. He says that when people watch him run they see a fullback coming down the field—but this fullback is fast and can run long.

He realizes that, at six feet and 180 pounds, he won't be a great marathoner; he knows that his open-water swimming is highly competitive; but he thinks that if he puts them all together, with his background, he can do well in a triple-event race. He has the natural capability and background to be a top athlete.

Dave is competitive. He wants to be a contender for the number one finishing spot. He realizes that success takes natural talent, training, skills, and the mental discipline to know pacing, to know how to listen to the body and the information that it is providing. This requires athletic maturity. According to Dave, the triathlon is a sport for older athletes who know their limits, their bodies, their ability to slow down or speed up according to their physiological state.

Why does Dave Horning compete in triathlons? "Personal self-worth, self-accomplishment. I can go out and be competitive in business, but that isn't my goal in life, because that has to do with other people and is not an individual accomplishment. When I participate in sports it is me, period. Nobody else. Sure, I want to win triathlons, but I am really competing against myself, my own personal goals."

Dave has the ability to inspire others as well as himself. His loves are sports, family, and his four dogs. To fit all this into his life is time consuming. When asked how he does it, he responds, "What is three hours a day? If it is important enough, you will find the time to train." His wife, Jan, is an athlete. She is up and swimming every morning and meets Dave in the hot tub in the evening. They have an agreement that he can seriously train for the Hawaii race this year and maybe the next as well.

Dave Scott (Davis, California)
Age: 28
Winner, 1980 International Ironman Triathlon
Winner, 1982 UTST San Diego Triathlon
Winner, October 1982 Ironman Triathlon World Championship

When the movie contracts are ready, Dave Scott will be signed as leading man. As with athlete-stars Johnny Weissmuller, Mark Spitz, and Buster Crabbe, Dave has the personality of the celebrity winner. With his relaxed manner, bright brown eyes, blond hair, 6-foot height, and 165 pounds of powerful frame, he is picture-perfect. Even more, he can talk intelligently. His background in exercise physiology comes through in discussions about overtraining, glycogen depletion, and mental discipline.

Dave is a hero in his hometown. He was raised in Davis, was educated for all of his years in Davis, and swam for Davis (university and city). He took up running in 1978 and cycling just months

Dave Scott—1980 and 1982 IRONMAN Triathlon World Championship Winner.

before his first Hawaii triathlon in 1980. He lettered in high school basketball, swimming, and water polo. In college he swam the 500 and 1,650 freestyle and played water polo on a team that did quite well, for a Division II college. In 1974, while majoring in physical education, he became the head coach of the fledgling Davis Masters Swim program, which grew from 6 to 400 participants under his tutelage.

Dave feels that swimmers have the greatest psychological advantage in training for triathlons. His years of swimming preparation taught him the following: to train virtually alone, in an enclosed space, with limited creativity during the workout, regardless of the weather conditions, for endless hours, seeing only one sight—the bottom of the pool. With this background he understood the discipline required to concentrate on other sports; he knew the value of a transference of attitude, rather than just motor skills or endurance.

Dave's two sisters were age-group swimmers. His mother and father both were completely supportive, attended their events, encouraged their excellence. Because of Dave's involvement with Masters' swimming, both of Dave's parents have made a commitment to fitness, something he is proud of because they now can follow their own athletic careers as well as their children's. His parents went to Hawaii with him as part of his crew, and they directed the Davis Triathlon for a number of years.

He decided in June 1979 to enter Hawaii's Ironman contest when he read the *Sports Illustrated* article on the event that year. He had never run a marathon, and he had never ridden his bike except around the streets of town. He knew little about training for the sport, other than the need to do a lot of swimming, biking, and running. He ran his first marathon that September in 2:45, which he feels was "satisfactory," and started biking later that same month. He won the Hawaii International Triathlon with a time of nine hours and 24 minutes. There wasn't another competitor who finished within an hour of his time, and *"ABC's Wide World of Sports"* followed Dave for the entire distance. The show and the trophies were his.

After Hawaii he was charged up. He decided to run more and traumatized a fatigued knee, developing chrondromalacia. After four months of little training he slowly got back into the sport, again winning the Davis Triathlon (a 10-K run, 20-mile ride, 1 1/2-mile swim) and setting a new course record of 1 hour and 56 minutes. He went into training for the 1981 Hawaii event but, plagued by knee problems, decided not to return to defend his title. Instead, he had to watch 1980's third-place finisher, John Howard, win the glory and steal the camera's eye.

Dave selects his races carefully, knowing that to win you cannot extend yourself in every triathlon competition. At the USTS race in San Diego (2-K, 35-K, 15-K), he dusted the men's field, finishing four minutes ahead of Scott Molina and Scott Tinley.

There is one significant point that you remember from talking with Dave Scott: "No one can train as hard as I can." That is probably true. He quit his job as the Masters Swim Coach in June 1981 to train full-time for triathlon competition. After five to eight hours of training per day he sleeps on tired muscles and dreams of winning the Ironman again in record time. Why would anyone dedicate his personal and professional life to the triathlon in Hawaii? Perhaps he knows the sport is coming of age and its victors will be rewarded with much more than trophies.

Scott speaks with reserve about training, feeling that his techniques must be well guarded so that he will have an edge on the competition. His training program is mapped out for the entire period according to mileage and workouts, but he changes the schedule to accommodate daily realities: the weather, his kinesthetic feeling, and his self-testing. He tests himself all the time. "I think you need to. Especially on the bicycling. I keep track of all my times, no matter the day or the workout." How important is it to train the distance of the race, such as Hawaii, on a regular basis? "I do not think it is critical or wise to do ultradistance triathlons comparable to Hawaii. Clearly, that distance should be done separately prior to the race, with a steady progression of miles in your minitriathlon efforts."

Dave's interest in triathletics is professional as well as avocational. He helps other triathletes design their programs, improve their performances, and prepare themselves psychologically for the race.

He has coached all his life and loves sports, so being a "triathlon consultant" is an extension of his already well-developed skills. He invites people who would like to use his professional consulting service to contact him. He teaches classes, conducts seminars, and writes on the subject.

Dave feels that the hardest part of an ultratriathlon is the psychological difficulty of dealing with distance and time. In a race such as Hawaii's, "As you get over the long bike leg, you are really stiff; and if you think of the run as a marathon, it is very difficult. If you think of it as just three hours more of a race that you have to endure, it becomes much easier." His interest in the race comes from the challenges that it presents plus the workouts required to develop conditioning. He enjoys long races and seeing the competition wear out. Where other athletes might seek to be the fastest or strongest, Dave wants to be the most enduring.

Dave is a vegetarian, eating on a regular basis "a tremendous amount of fruit, rice, potatoes, bulgur." He practices a prerace glycogen-loading program, which he describes as one "that consists of eating slightly more than your normal intake of glycogen 1 1/2 days prior to the race. Then there is the super-compensation diet which is protein and fat three to four days before, followed by loading up three days before the race on carbohydrates." He feels that too many competitors eat too much sucrose (sugar), both while they train and while they race, and treat the race as if it were an eight-course meal, eating constantly.

Dave has had his problems with injuries. It seems that they plague him after the events. He cautions triathletes to listen to their bodies during training, which he admits is easier said than done. He recommends that all triathletes stretch to increase the flexibility of the muscles needed to run after dismounting the bicycle and suggests that single-sport athletes train with weights to increase the strength in their underdeveloped triple-sport musculature.

Dave agrees that there is a triathlon boom right now, but he predicts that it will not surpass the numbers of people who have turned to running or swimming because of the need to train in three sports. He would like to see the development of age-division triathlons as an alternative to single-event and team-sport emphasis.

Although Dave has quit his job to train full-time, he still reserves time for a social life. His family and friends are all supportive of his goal: to be the best triathlete. In workouts he is usually alone. "I want to train on my own schedule rather than try to fit into someone else's time requirement." If at 10:00 A.M. he needs to ride for four hours, he simply doesn't want to put it off for a few hours so that he can have companionship. Those long years in the pool have taught him self-reliance and the ability to continue solo.

The competitive side of Dave Scott might best be described as reserved, yet eager for that day in October when he can meet the challenge he has set for himself. Dave is one of the few people to commit unstintingly to the task of total aerobic fitness, to developing his body to its maximum strength, speed, and endurance in three sports. As in all competition, the investment carries risk. But with Dave's resilience and determination, the gold medals are there for the taking.

Eva Oberth-Olson (Fair Oaks, California)
Age: 24
Winner, 1981 Sierra Nevada Triathlon

Eva is one of those naturally gifted athletes: strong, quick, and tall (5' 9'' and 160 pounds). She was blessed with a great love of sports and learned to participate in many with proficiency: ski mountaineering, kayaking, backpacking, hiking, water polo, and water skiing in addition to biking, running, and swimming. She can be described as an adventure athlete, yet she loves the excitement of competition and has the spirit of winning in her blood.

Her background includes family involvement in outdoor recreational sports. With her parents, older brother, and younger sister ever active, Eva feels that she has been conditioned all of her life for triathlons. In her youth her folks stabled a horse miles away from home, and she commuted by bike every day to ride and care for the animal. She says, "I've been doing sports like that ever since

Eva Oberth-Olsen—Winner 1981 Lodi and Sierra Nevada Triathlon and 1982 Turlock Triathlon Winner.

I was three feet tall. Our whole family participated in backpacking and other outdoor fun.''

She liked to run as well and joined the boys' track team in high school, since there was none for girls. ''Being the only girl on the boys' team was a real drag,'' she remarks, ''because you never win.'' When she went on to college (California State University, Chico), she ran track and played water polo one year and field hockey for two years. Eva says that she was never the best athlete but ''maybe a little better than average, as I am a go-for-it type of person.'' Eva graduated with a teaching credential in physical education and a minor in English. Currently she is substitute teaching in high school while awaiting a contract opening.

Eva always ran to stay in shape for her other sports. Her one marathon effort was clocked at four hours and five minutes. Running is not her favorite sport! She considers herself a ''dedicated jogger—running is just real hard.'' She currently runs 30 miles a week, but her knee has been bothering her—not uncommon for triathletes in serious training.

She didn't swim on a team, but her water polo experience pays off. She is used to treading water and sprinting to the ball and is developing her endurance stroke.

Eva's cycling was done mostly for transportation. Each member of her family owned a Schwinn Varsity bicycle, and they often cycled together. ''We would easily do 60 miles in a day together. Never competitively; never in training.''

Her first triathlon was The Great Race in Sacramento in 1981, a bike/kayak/run contest, which she won. That same year she tackled a few more triathlons, winning three that summer. The Sierra Nevada Triathlon (two-mile swim, 50-mile ride, and 13.1-mile run) win earned her an airplane ticket to the February 1982 Ironman. There she finished as the eighth woman with a time of 12 hours and 13 minutes.

She has had difficulty staying on a crosstraining schedule. ''I had all of these great ambitions. Things happen. You become completely off schedule in one week, and you can't catch up.''

She is using the information from her physical education background as a guide in setting up a training program. By following her log, she keeps track of the changes ". . . just so that I can look and make sure that I am really not blowing it."

She feels the hardest part about a triathlon is the running "because it is the most tiring. If you are a good biker, you have an edge because it is the longest part, but if you are a good runner, that helps at the end." (This is the classic argument between the biker and runner as to which has the advantage; enter the swimmer and you have a three-way argument.)

Eva has that infectious type of laugh that is so appealing. It is important in the field of sports competition to have a sharpened sense of humor. Yet, she says "I tend to be real hard on myself; I really get down on myself, like when my running isn't going well." She suspects that her sense of discipline could be improved and in the next breath admits, "If you are not hard on yourself, it is difficult to be productive." She acknowledges that pushing herself keeps her in touch with herself, focuses her inward. Nonetheless, when it comes down to answering "Why do you do it?" the truth comes out: Eva simply has a lot of fun in sports. She enjoys participating.

Eva is an example of a different kind of triathlete from Dave Scott, who has the drive and the desire to train "harder than anyone else in the United States," and Dave Horning, who has a strong enough background in all three sports to be a contender. Eva is even more than a triple-fitness athlete; she is an all-around athlete. She loves all sports and participates in most; and she is extraordinary in everything that she attempts. She has the spirit that more determined athletes sometimes lack—a freedom to love every moment and to share this feeling with others. Eva is a triathlete and then some.

organizing a triathlon

By Bill Thomas
Race Director
Sierra Nevada Triathlon

The skill and self-discipline required for the triathlete in balancing his efforts in this triple-sport event make it more challenging than any other athletic contest.—Fletcher Hanks, Race Director, International Oxford Triathlon

A triathlon is logistically more complex than other races because race organizers must prepare for three consecutive events plus two transitions. The key to success is in planning, delegating, and following up. The race director must choose qualified committee members and manage the race organization as "chairman of the board." The director who tries to run the whole show is destined to fail.

THE RACE ORGANIZATION

The race organization should consist of a race director and board members who are assigned specific, realistic responsibilities. The organization for the Sierra Nevada Triathlon, held at Folsom Lake near Sacramento in early September, consists of the race director, four race coordinators, and numerous support coordinators. The four race coordinators are each responsible for their major

The race director's dream—the finish line.

segments: the swim, the bike, the run, and the transitions. Coordinators should be highly qualified in their specialties, i.e., open-water swimmers, bicycle racers, runners and triathletes (who understand the importance of smooth transitions). Many communities have clubs or teams that specialize in each sport. For example, the Sierra Nevada Triathlon race coordinators consist of the Sacramento Masters Swimmers, the Sacramento Golden Wheelmen, Fleet Feet Running Club, and two experienced triathletes for the transitions. The real spirit of the sport comes through when experts plan each event.

The race director's job is to keep the four coordinators on time schedules and to ensure that the race segments are comparable in quality. The director must also ensure that the coordinators have as much free rein as possible and that there is little discord within the organization.

The support coordinators' responsibilities should include registra-

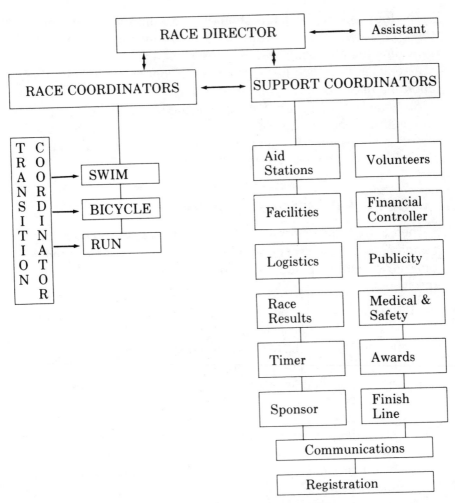

Triathlon Race Organizational Chart

tion, timing, finish line, medical, public relations, awards, aid procurement and distribution, equipment, race results, typing and printing, communication, volunteers, prerace packet, notifying local authorities, status boards, advertising, entry forms, and photography.

The four race coordinators should be responsible for designing the course (with the race director's help), marking the course, providing the aid required during the race, and supervising their segments on race day. Just as the director depends on them, the coordinators must rely on their assistants.

An organizational chart that explains the race committee structure is shown below. It is designed to help you realize the complexity of sponsoring such an event, as well as to help you delegate the job responsibilities required.

MAJOR RACE DIRECTOR'S DECISIONS

There are certain decisions that you must make as you plan your triathlon. You should set priorities for your event. Answering these questions might help you clarify the major issues that need to be resolved:

1. Is your race to be designed for mass participation, for extreme degree of difficulty, and/or for fun?
2. Is the race budgeted as a fundraising, profit-making, or publicity-generating event?
3. Are the facilities available to make each of the three events balanced in distance and difficulty?
4. Is the concern of all persons present to make the race an event designed for the benefit of the athlete rather than the race promotors, sponsors, and media?
5. Is your first and foremost concern the safety of all participants and spectators?
6. Is the race planned to the satisfaction of all the competitors, not just the top few who receive the press limelight?
7. Have you decided that the race will be *fun* for all participants, and have you provided those elements of fun?
8. Is your primary commitment to ensure that the race is thoroughly organized, with complete planning and attention paid to all detail?
9. Are you willing to work with the committee/board of directors structure and delegate both duties and power?

Incoming and outgoing plan for a properly designed bicycle course.

10. Are you a "people person," able to generate enthusiasm from all around you to participate both as a contestant and as a race volunteer?

SELECTING A COURSE

The race director should determine the race distances and course layout. Consider the time of year and avoid scheduling conflicts. (You don't want to have the bicycle race go through a parade or have the swim course planned for a time when the water level of the lake will be lower than normal by 20 feet). It seems to be most convenient for contestants, crews, and spectators if the start and finish of all events are in the same area. This is not essential, however, and depends on other factors, such as course length and availability of facilities. Some triathlons employ a point-to-point concept in order to combine challenging race segments. For example, the Escape from Alcatraz triathlon is a combination of a swim from Alcatraz Island to San Francisco, a bicycle ride across the Golden Gate Bridge into Mill Valley, and the Double Dipsea run—from Mill Valley over the mountains to the Pacific Ocean and back.

The course should be well marked and should have accessible aid stations. Consider checkpoint locations. Since each event is likely to include novice contestants, safety is a paramount concern when laying out a course. If possible, design the swim so that the contestants will be visible at all times and close to shore or assistance (buoys, boats, etc.). Similarly, the bike course should be as free as possible from traffic and sharp, fast turns. Require that all contestants wear protective headgear. When designing a bike course along roads, consider the time of day for the race, alternate routes, and the direction of travel—have contestants travel on the busiest roads when the car traffic is lightest.

Don't forget to take the weather into account. Generally, the earlier the start, the better, particularly in events that will last only a few hours. In ultradistance events, especially if the run is the final event, try to schedule your triathlon so that contestants can run in the cooler, early evening hours.

Contrary to popular belief, there are no established distances for triathlons. Terms like half-triathlon (meaning half the Hawaii triathlon in distance) are not precise. Each race is a full triathlon, requiring different skill levels, conditioning, and race tactics. Some are sprints; others are true tests of endurance. If the coordinators want to stage an unbiased multiple-sport test, then they must design courses for each that are comparable in the energy, effort, fitness, and ability that they require. One way to determine equal time differentials is to calculate how much time there will be between the fastest and the average competitors in each event. Using this concept, a one-hour swim could have the same spread between the fastest and the average competitors as would a three-hour bicycle portion or a two-hour run, depending on the course conditions and the order of the events. (There is no "correct" order of events, but safety considerations should be a prime factor in determining the sequence.)

Course design is the ultimate responsibility of the race director. He or she must ensure that each event flows smoothly into the next and that each is safe, challenging, and fun to watch. The spectators' as well as the athletes' needs should always play a part in the final decisions about the race.

TIMETABLE OF ACTIVITIES

To plan and run a highly successful triathlon, proper planning must be foremost in your mind. Below is a flow chart of activities to be organized prior to the race and a timing sequence that ensures that your race will run smoothly. It is absolutely necessary to form a race committee that will work hard, accept responsibility, demonstrate follow-through, and enjoy the rewards of volunteering—the pride of knowing that the athletes will race in a beautifully orchestrated event!

Nine to Twelve Months Prior

Select a race director. Discuss basic race concepts, course possibilities, budget, and goals.

Six to Nine Months Prior

The race director selects race coordinators. Seek sponsorship. Establish a race headquarters. Design a course. Meet as a committee. Develop an outline of race requirements. Establish a budget. Prepare an entry form. Mail the entry form and information to periodicals and athletes. Fund a checking account. Notify the proper authorities and obtain necessary permits.

Four to Six Months Prior

Select support coordinators. Meet as a full committee to discuss the race concept, the race management, and the team approach.

Specially designed bicycle racks keep the frames in an upright position and in numerical sequence.

Review the budget, modifying it as necessary. Establish responsibilities and time schedules. Mail entry forms to contestants and distribute them to specialty retail stores. Develop a checklist for each race coordinator and begin to track progress.

Two to Three Months Prior

Complete and mail the prerace packet to participants as they register. Meet as a full committee—go through the checklist to ensure that all race coordinators' needs are filled by support coordinators. Order and make race supplies (aid, cups, numbers, awards, signs, etc.). Again review the budget. Remind local authorities of the event. Write a press release, taking media headlines into account.

One Week to One Month Prior

Mark the course. Sponsor a clinic and practice runs. Review the budget and modify again, if necessary. Meet with the full committee or race coordinators as required.

Three Days to One Week Prior

Prepare the final list of entrants. Talk with the coordinators. Organize all the equipment and supplies required.

One or Two Days Prior

Mark the course the final time. Review checklists. Sponsor a social get-together, a bicycle check-in, a meeting of the press.

Race Day

Be available to answer questions and solve problems. Be calm and cool all day!

One Day to Three Weeks After

Compile and mail the race results. Sponsor a race committee celebration.

As triathlons grow in popularity and participation, it will be necessary for those who have experience as contestants to volunteer to help in this massive organizational scheme. It is important to remember that, if you have been on the receiving end (as a participant), it is only fair to pay your dues back to your sport. Help by volunteering at a race.

To all race directors, who must conduct such a symphony of three sports simultaneously, I wish good luck and hope that the mistakes don't show, that the rain doesn't fall, and that the entrants have a truly wonderful experience.

17

ultradistance triathlons: the price of admission

Athletes, like investment brokers, need to weigh their costs in training against the return of their performance. The costs of performance include all the golden energy, commitment, hours of training, sacrifices, joy, and pain that the race demands. The benefits of the performance are simply measured: how well you did in the race.

In the past we had no accurate way to analyze what the energy cost of a performance was, especially for long-distance performance. We now complicate matters by attempting to analyze the costs of performance in three sports considered in sequence. Doing well (or, doing better) in an athletic event means trying to extend your capacity to function at a high level of exertion.

FATIGUE

Fatigue is a self-regulating response of the body that prevents injury due to overexertion—the screeching, painful process whereby the body applies its own set of brakes to prevent self-destruction. The body shuts down, limiting its own capacity to do work.

Fatigue is still not completely understood. Many physiological factors, which change during continuous exercise, may contribute

Claire McCarty, a 25-year-old from Santa Monica and 1982 women's winner of the Lake Castiac Triathlon, feels that slow, screeching, painful process whereby the body applies its own set of brakes against itself—fatigue.

to the state known as fatigue. These include dehydration; hypoglycemia; lactic acid accumulation; variation in blood acidity and alkalinity, pyruvate levels, ion (salt) levels; cardiorespiratory dynamics, and many others. The single factor that correlates most consistently with the onset of fatigue, however, is muscle-glycogen depletion. When muscle-glycogen stores drop below about three grams per kilogram of muscle tissue, the athlete experiences extreme fatigue. (Normal muscle has about 18 grams of glycogen per kilogram of muscle tissue. The process of glycogen loading may increase this to as much as 45 grams of glycogen per kilogram of muscle tissue.) Muscle-glycogen depletion causes fatigue, especially in endurance events of four hours and longer, for two reasons: it is a primary fuel source, and it cannot be replaced as fast as it is depleted. Muscle-glycogen depletion is responsible for the runner's "wall" and the cyclist's "bonk."

Wonderful, Wonderful Glycogen!

During the 1981 International Ironman Triathlon, an ultratriathlon distance, one of my concerns was being able to complete the event. To my amazement, I found that the 2.4-mile open-water swim was relatively easy (since I paced myself reasonably) and that I was fresh as I boarded my two-wheeler and cycled ahead on the 112-mile ride over the humid, scorching, unshaded highway. I wasn't surprised to find that I was slowing down as the hours passed, especially once the cycling segment was finished. One of the first noticeable changes that occurs when you stop cycling and start running takes place because the muscle sets that are used are similar yet opposing. They are the same muscles, but the directions they must move in are different. The change requires an adjustment and is awkward at first. Slowly your legs fall into the rhythm that they know from so many miles of running. At the halfway point of the marathon, I crumbled—I was reduced to a combination of running for one mile and walking for one minute. My fatigue was so deep that this was the maximum energy that I could muster to continue the race.

Exercise physiologists could clearly describe what was taking place. As I burned muscle glycogen, I also made use of the other fuel sources that the muscles have available: blood-borne glucose, glycogen stored in the liver, and free fatty acids. The four sources of energy work together. However, they provide different amounts of calories and burn at different rates. Toward the end of the race my performance needs were greater than my body's ability to provide the nutrients and calories stored in these fuels. The result was fatigue. I was able to continue, but my abilities had so diminished that I was performing at a fraction of my optimal capacity.

Efficient glycogen utilization is the key to continuing to perform at a high level. Glycogen is stored in the muscle tissue and cannot be released into the bloodstream. You have a specific amount of glycogen stored in your muscles when you begin a race; as you burn this amount to lower levels, your body signals the muscles to start using more blood-borne glucose and free fatty acids as major fuel sources.

In the digestive process, carbohydrates are broken down into simple sugars and then carried from the intestinal tract to the bloodstream and to the liver. In the liver these simple sugars are converted to glucose in the form of blood-borne glucose. Some of the simple sugars (a small amount) are changed to glycogen, which is then stored by the muscle or liver.

Glycogen is wonderful because it carries more useful energy per liter of oxygen than any other fuel source. For every liter of oxygen, glycogen delivers 5.01 calories, compared with fat, which delivers 4.65 calories. Glycogen, then, is a high-octane fuel. This is especially important during endurance events, which require that the available oxygen be converted to work as efficiently as possible.

Fat, on the other hand, is best used for lower-intensity exercise. As the intensity of the activity increases, more glycogen is needed to maintain a consistently high level of performance. Ultimately, glycogen stores determine your performance.

Most athletes, without consciously realizing the process, are training their metabolism to be efficient, as well as training their muscles to become swift and strong. The training process has the remarkable effect of improving the athlete's ability to remove metabolic wastes, to increase the levels of muscle enzymes, and to improve the body's ability to utilize fatty acids sooner and at a higher threshold. Trained athletes have taught their systems to spare glycogen and utilize fat.

Glycogen is an irreplaceable resource within the time frame of the race. It simply cannot be replaced at the rate that it is being consumed, though, if you eat, it is being replaced at a slower rate. Look at the Decrease in Glycogen Stores graph.

This graph clearly shows that if an athlete exercises at 120 percent of his max VO_2 (maximum oxygen uptake), he becomes exhausted within minutes. In this situation, since the stores of glycogen are high, the cause of exhaustion is the anaerobic demand on the cir-

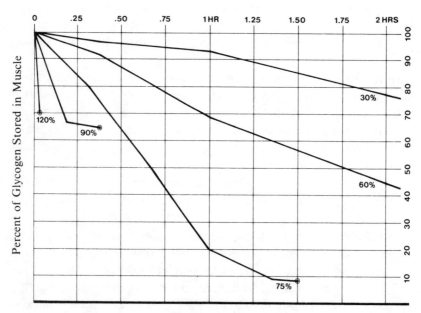

Time in Hours

⊛ = Point of Exhaustion
% = Percent of VO^2

Decrease in Glycogen Stores

culorespiratory system, not the depletion of glycogen. At the 90-percent VO_2 level, again we see that exhaustion occurs in less than 30 minutes, though high levels of glycogen still remain. If you exercise at 75 percent of your maximum VO_2, exhaustion probably will be caused by depletion of stored glycogen at the 1½-hour mark.

The exhaustion point coincides with the extremely low muscle-glycogen levels. Between the 60 percent and 89 percent max VO_2, the depletion of glycogen seems to be the limiting factor restricting performance.

When glycogen stores diminish far enough, you fail. Some people can continue to function slowly at very low glycogen levels. Their fatty-acid metabolism cycle and new synthesis of glucose by the liver can continue to keep them going at some lower exertion rate, say, 60 percent of maximum. The better trained you are, the longer you can perform at higher levels of ability, because you can efficiently utilize several fuel sources.

The reason that this graph stops at 120 minutes is that experiments have not been done beyond this time period. Researchers have not put athletes on treadmills for longer periods of time and have not taken muscle biopsies periodically to assess the available percentage of muscle glycogen. Endurance athletes are performing "experiments" in the field, so to speak; our conclusions about the factors that limit performance after the two-hour mark must therefore remain tentative.

For ultradistance performance the implications of existing research are numerous. You can improve your glycogen utilization by training your metabolism. Also, if you can store greater amounts of glycogen (say, by carbohydrate loading), the lines of the graph will change. Because triathletes use three different major muscle groups, and measurements are taken in the specific muscles used, you should be able to perform at different percentages of your max VO_2 in different sports, depending on their crossover effect.

Unfortunately, when you discover that you are fatigued in the race, it is too late. You are already so far behind the eight ball that

Bananas are some of the foods that propel triathletes because they contain a high percentage of carbohydrate calories.

you can't get out of the glycogen-depletion hole. That is why it is critical to assess your ability prior to the race and to learn at what levels you can perform. This requires that you start at a reasonable pace so that you won't run out of your reserves. Your self-testing and time trials will help. You have to test to find out your strengths and weaknesses. They will tell you not only what kind of effect your training has had but how you can change your program to increase the training effect.

How do you decide what percentage of your maximum to perform at in each event? It is difficult to assess and measure at exactly what level you are capable of performing. Rather, my intention is to give you a handle on the different types of information that you must consider. You can use this information to gauge how well your training is going, how hard you are pushing in all three different sports.

CALORIC COSTS OF PERFORMANCE

A series of charts has been developed to demonstrate the relationship between the number of calories expended in cycling and running (see pages 260–261). The factors that affect caloric requirements are metabolic rate, age, weight, and speed. Particularly in cycling, the major consideration to the cost of the exercise is your speed. As you cycle faster, wind resistance increases geometrically, making you work disproportionately harder and thereby increasing your energy requirements.

To give you a ball-park idea of the relationship between the three triathlon events and caloric expenditure, suppose that the following conditions exist: An individual weighs 150 pounds and finishes the International Triathlon in Hawaii with these results: he swims 2.4 miles in 1½ hours, cycles 112 miles in 7 hours, and runs 26.2 miles in 4 hours—a total elapsed time of 12½ hours. Knowing these basics, you can estimate the energy expenditure as follows:

1. **Swim:** 4.5 calories per pound of body weight at a speed of 2 miles per hour expends 814 calories
2. **Cycle:** 7 hours on a 25-pound 10-speed expends 2,660 calories
3. **Run:** a 26.2-mile marathon in 4 hours expends 2,699 calories

The results:

Swim	814 calories	or	13%
Cycle	2,660 calories	or	43%
Run	2,699 calories	or	44%
TOTAL	6,173 calories	or	100%

The analysis will change with people of different body weights and biomechanical efficiency. The point here is to give you an idea of the relationship between the caloric costs for individual events.

The energy costs of a triathlon are specific to that triathlon because of differences in the course, terrain, temperatures, distances, and other factors. Thus, the finishing times of triathlons cannot be meaningfully compared to each other. The caloric costs

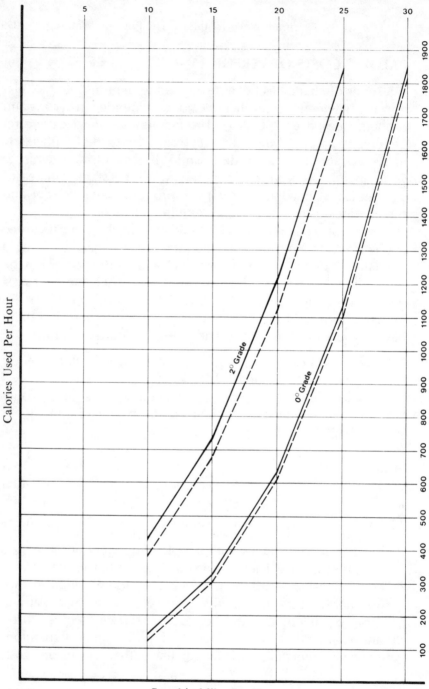

Caloric Cost of Cycling.

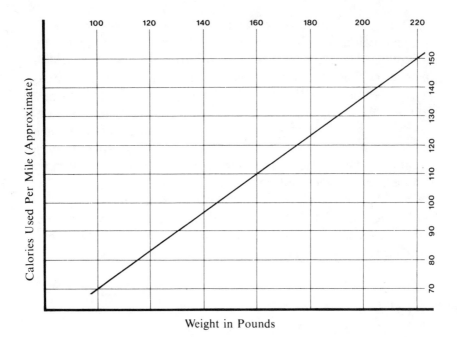

Caloric Cost of Running.

of the race must be computed separately for each event. A workbook approach is used so that you can follow the simple arithmetic of measuring the mets, or energy required, to complete each event: the run, the bicycle, and the swim. The met charts in Chapter 5 will be used for this exercise.

It is our intent, then, to calculate the mets required to perform at a specific pace for a specific distance and then to convert that figure into an oxygen capacity that can be compared to a maximum capacity to show you at what percentage of your maximum capacity you are capable of performing. Since you know that you can continue to do work for extended periods of time if you perform at less than 100 percent of your maximum, you can then determine how long you can continue to perform at that rate before you "bonk" or "hit the wall."

STOP! If you expect to finish a triathlon in less than three hours, the race will probably not deplete your glycogen stores. It's not important to you to compute performance costs—read no further. In races of that distance, the fuel source is not the crucial factor in completing the triathlon at a high level of performance, because you are not being required to perform aerobically for extended periods of time. Rather, some of the limiting factors are the ability of your muscles to contract rapidly, their oxygen-carrying capabilities, and your body's ability to remove the waste by-products of the metabolism.

GO! If you predict your finishing time to be more than three hours, you need to complete this workbook so that you can determine just how to maximize your performance and conserve your fuel supply to make it through the long events.

ULTRATRIATHLON WORK EQUATIONS

This workbook is designed for you to fill in. To assist you, I've included a hypothetical example.

1. *Question:* What are the distances of each of the events in the triathlon?

       You   —   **Example**

Swim____Bike____Run____   Swim _2 mi_ Bike _50 mi_ Run _13.1 mi_

2. *Question:* What are your projected finish time goals?

       You   **Example**

Swim____Bike____Run____   Swim _1 hr_ Bike _3 hrs_ Run _95 min_

3. *Question:* What is your dry-land absolute weight in pounds converted to kilograms?

You

_____lbs ÷ 2.24 = _____Kilograms (kg)

Example

_120_ lbs ÷ 2.24 = _54_ Kilograms (kg)

4. *Question:* What are the results in mets of your self-test in each event?

	You			**Example**	
	Time	*Mets*		*Time*	*Mets*
Swim	_____	_____		6:53	13.0
Bike	_____	_____		8:15	13.0
Run	_____	_____		8:35	17.0

5. *Question:* What is your highest met score?

You		**Example**	
Sport	Met	Sport	Met
_____	_____	Run	17.0

6. *Question:* Can you convert mets to the amount of oxygen used if 1 met = 3.5 ml O_2/kg/minute?

You

_____×_____kg × 3.5 = _____ml of oxygen used

Example

_17_ × _54_ kg × 3.5 = _3.213_ ml of oxygen used

7. *Question:* Can you convert this figure to maximum oxygen uptake (Max VO_2)?

You

_____ml O_2 ÷_____kg =_____ml O_2/kg

Example

___3.213___ ml O_2 ÷___54___kg = ___59.5___ml O_2/kg

Your maximum oxygen uptake is_____ml O_2/kg

Go to Chapter 6 and see results from self-test.

©Norman L. Jones et al. *CLINICAL EXERCISE TESTING.* Philadelphia: Saunders, 1975, pg. 12.

8. *Question:* Are your goals reasonable?

RUN GOAL

You   **Example**

_____minutes   ___95___minutes

a. What is your pace per mile for that goal?

You

_____min ÷ 13.1 mi. =_____

Example

___95___min ÷ 13.1 mi. = _7:15_ min./mile

b. How long will it take you to run 1½ miles?

You

_____ × 1.5 =_____min_____sec

Example

_7¼_ × 1.5 = _10_min_52_sec

c. What is your met requirement at this pace (see Chapter 6, Table 1)

You	**Example**
_____mets	_13.5_ mets

d. At what percent of your maximum met capacity are you working? (Formula is your pace in mets divided by your maximum capacity times 100.)

You

_____ = _____ %

Example

_13.5/17_ = _79.4_ %

e. How many minutes can you run at 79 percent of maximum? (See Decrease in Glycogen Stores graph.)

You	**Example**
approx._____	approx. _100 min._

f. If you ran the distance in your goals of (a)_____ minutes with glycogen stores lasting (b)_____ minutes, will you have enough fuel to complete the race at that percentage? (If a is greater than b.)_____ Yes   (If b is greater than a.)_____No

BICYCLE GOAL

You	**Example**
_____minutes	_1½ hrs/180_ minutes

a. What is your pace per mile for that goal?

You

_____min. ÷ _____miles = _____

Example

_180_ min ÷ _50_ miles = 3 min/mile

b. How long will it take you to ride 3 miles at this pace?

You

_____ × 3 miles = _____

Example

_3_ × 3 miles = _9_

c. What is your met requirement at this pace? (See Chapter 6, Table 2.)

You	**Example**
_____mets	_12_ mets

d. At what percentage of your maximum met capacity are you working? (See Question 4.)

You

_____pace in mets ÷ _____max capacity = _____%

Example

_12_ pace in mets ÷ _17_ max capacity = _71_ %

e. How many minutes can you cycle at this percentage of maximum? (See Decrease in Glycogen Stores graph.)

You	Example
____hours	_3-4_ hours

f. If you cycle this distance of your goal of _180_ minutes with glycogen stores lasting _180_ minutes, will you have enough fuel to complete the race at that percentage?

You	Example
____Yes____No	✔ barely Yes____No

SWIM GOAL

You	Example
____minutes	_60_ minutes

a. What is your pace per yard for that goal?

You

____yards ÷ ____min. = ____

Example

_3,520_ yards ÷ _60_ min. = _58.7_

b. How long will it take you to swim 400 yards at this pace?

You

400 yards × ____pace = ____

Example

400 yards × _58.7_ pace = _6.82 min._

c. What is your met requirement at this pace? (See Chapter 6, Table 3.)

You	**Example**
_____mets	_13_ mets

d. At what percentage of your maximum capacity are you working? (Formula is to divide your pace in mets by your maximum capacity and multiply by 100.)

You	**Example**
= _____%	$\frac{13}{17}$ = _76_ %

e. How many minutes can you swim at this percentage of maximum? (See Decrease in Glycogen Stores graph.)

You	**Example**
_____minutes	_90_ minutes

f. If you swim this distance in your goal of_____/ 60 minutes with glycogen store lasting_____/ 90 minutes, will you have enough fuel to complete the race at that percentage?

You	**Example**
_____Yes_____No	_✔_ Yes_____No
	Probably should try a faster pace.

9. *Question:* Can you compare the three sports at the percentages of their maximum met capacity?

	COMBINATION SUMMARY		TIME SUMMARY	
	You	**Example**	**You**	**Example**
Swim	____ %	76 %	____	1
Bike	____ %	71 %	____	3
Run	____ %	79 %	____	1.5
			Total ____	5.5 hrs.

10. *Question:* Can you continue to perform at those percentages of maximum met capacity for that amount of time?

____ Yes ____ No (See Decrease in Glycogen Stores graph.)

When this is all tied together, a synthesis of three performance evaluations in three different sports, you have an approximate finish time based on your own capacity to work rather than on speculation. It is not precise; it is simply a method to give you a feel for the task at hand. Once you have participated in a few triathlons you can compare your actual split times to your calculated times and make appropriate adjustments in your pacing in each event.

18

tips for triathletes

The lessons learned from experience carry a special kind of weight, a particular kind of authority. Experience can be a costly way to learn about triathlons, but the lessons learned this way seem to be the most firmly embedded. They simply are not forgotten easily.

When I was training for the 1981 Ironman Triathlon, it seemed like a reasonable idea to attempt each separate event in the triathlon on three successive days. It was only after I experienced this kind of training that I realized that it was a valuable concept for several reasons: it let me try out the equipment I would be using; it was a measure of the effectiveness of my training to that point; and it was a simulation of actual race conditions. It proved to be a valuable triathlon tip.

Because of the lack of available research on crosstraining, tips on how to improve performance in triathlons must come from the "school of triathlon experience." I hope that any ideas I have to offer will save you pain, offer you gain, and keep you sane, since the quest for triple fitness makes significant demands on many parts of our lives.

TIME BUDGETING

Training for triathlons—the triathlon lifestyle—truly requires that you learn to deal with time. You will be asking yourself to juggle the time demands of training schedules, sleep requirements, pro-

270

Since you can't control the length of your life, you might as well have something to say about its width and depth.

fessional work, your family, and, finally, your own personal growth in a day that contains only 24 hours. Yet you may often feel that you now waste time, feeling (with or without justification) that you simply are not able to accomplish as much as you would like to in one day.

All successful triathletes must have a way of using and controlling their time and must know the value of it—this is called *time management*. Before we can explore this notion, we must first believe that there *is* enough time available: if a workday consists of eight hours, this means that there are three full eight-hour workdays in each 24-hour clock day. If you spend one eight-hour workday at an income-producing job, and you sleep away another eight-hour workday, you still have one bonus workday left to use as you wish—for training and other activities.

So, there *is* enough time. The next question is, can you manage time or does it manage you? The answer to this question is simple: you must set goals, design and use schedules to achieve those goals, and eliminate anything that threatens to disrupt the schedules and goals. Yes, it is easier to say this than to practice it, but I know from experience that it works.

Just as we cannot ride our bicycle from one place to another in a new territory without a detailed road map, we cannot advance in our triple-fitness lifestyle without a tri-fitness map. Making a tri-fitness map helps give you direction, purpose and organization. It helps you know what course to chart. A trifitness map requires that you simply sit down and decide where you want your fitness destination to be. Where do you want to be six months from now, five years from now, or farther into the future?

Fix your goals in writing. Post them on the refrigerator door or in your training log. Just seeing these objectives regularly will help you reach them faster. On my refrigerator at home is a timely newspaper article with the headline "BURP! Fatties Face Off For a Five-Hour Food Binge," which shows pictures of Dee Dee eating 42,194 calories and Big Bertha gobbling 36,692 calories within five hours' time. The purpose of the article is to keep me from opening the refrigerator door and turning into one of those two professional fatsos.

You must set a target time for when you plan to reach these goals. The tri-fitness map shown below will be useful in helping you determine the direction in which you are going. In addition, it is useful to set weekly, monthly and yearly goals for yourself. I usually list a self-test, a race, or an upcoming fun-triathlon. I also recommend that you delineate your life priorities. List what is most important to you—it is absurd to train and work hard if it costs you your health, your family, or your friends. So pay attention to what you write down and make yourself aware of it frequently.

Tri-fitness Map

My Life Priorities:

1.

2.

3.

4.

5.

6.

7.

8.

9.

10.

My Most Significant/Important Sports Accomplishment to Date:

X Starting Point

Date: **Accomplishment**
My Goals: **1 month**

Continued on next page.

Date: Accomplishment
My Goals   6 months

Date: Accomplishment
My Goals: 1 year

Date: Accomplishment
My Goals: 3–5 years

   During my 20 years of athletic competition in a variety of sports, I have had the opportunity to meet highly successful athletes and health-oriented professionals. There are many reasons why these people are successful, but they share two common traits: the ability to organize and the ability to focus their energy. They like order, discipline, and specific game-planning. They leave little to chance, to winging it. They tend to be the type of people who make lists, for they know that 10 minutes of planning can save them four hours of squandered time. For some, this means that their entire day will be planned, that all of their objectives will be written down.

   Sure, there will be booby traps. Even after you develop discipline and focus, outside influences will be eager to disrupt your plans. Booby traps are the inevitable obstacles in an active athlete's life.

   One last note on how to manage time in your life, especially as you become more involved with training for a time-consuming event like a triathlon: you must realize that each of us relates to time in a different way. Referees *call* time; prisoners *serve* time;

musicians *mark* time; historians *record* time; loafers *kill* time; statisticians *keep* time; athletes *race* against time. But no matter how you relate to time, the fact remains that we are all given exactly the same amount of time. There are 24 hours in a day, 168 hours in a week. Use them. Use them fully—live every moment.

RACE POINTERS

There are certain techniques, tactics, and strategies that you can use to improve your performance in the actual triathlon race. You've used most of these strategies in your experience as a single-sport specialist. Now you can apply them to multi-event races. By paying attention to detail, thinking through the race in advance, and considering what you must do after the race, you will find that the triathlon race itself is more enjoyable and that you will be able to finish higher in the pack.

Prerace Preparation

There is no substitute for proper training and the confidence that you develop when you enter an event knowing that you have followed a disciplined training plan. It is this preparation that produces self-esteem. As an important event draws near, there is no room for destructive self-doubt to enter the picture.

As the day of the race draws closer, however, it will become necessary to taper. You need to let your mind and body slow down and relax. There is no single approach to tapering that works best for everyone, though, so you must experiment. Doug Latimer, the 1981 co-winner of the Western States 100-Mile Endurance Run, once explained to me that his theory of tapering was to run his longest, hardest, toughest training run exactly two weeks before the race. (For him, this consisted of a 75-mile run through the roughest imaginable terrain.) For the next two weeks his plan was to run a few easy miles and stay loose. You need to find out how much and what kind of rest your body requires. Obviously, this

Scott Molina quickly eases on a pair of tricot running shorts over his lycra swim suit and is off on the bicycle stage.

will vary depending on the length of the events in the race.

Another important consideration is prerace diet. You are going to have to decide what foods and what pattern of eating will maximize the amount of stored-muscle glycogen in your body. Some people will choose to maintain their regular eating habits so as not to upset their gastrointestinal tract. Others will decide on a super-compensation glycogen-loading routine. Either way, you will probably notice that your weight will increase because you have switched to a calorie-burning system in which you are eating more and exercising less. Couple this with the fact that you are probably also hyperhydrating, and you might find that you are reaching new highs on the bathroom scale.

It's a good idea to drive or ride over the race course in advance to plan out each of the day's events in proper sequence—here you will use the *visualization techniques* you learned earlier. During this prerace course planning session, you will be able to decide what equipment you will need, the sections of the course on which you can either push it a bit or relax and coast, how to use the course to your best advantage, and how the competition will probably fare, and you will do other basic advance preparation of all your systems.

As you prepare your strategy, decide on your personal goals and expectations for the event. At the United States Triathlon Series– San Diego event in June 1982, I decided to run the race at about 85 percent of my full capacity in order to learn about the kind of race in which I was required to swim two kilometers, bicycle 35 kilometers, and run 15 kilometers—a middle-distance multisport event. My mental preparation, then, was not to place myself in the role of a contender for a winning spot in that race. Rather, my goals were to experience and learn from the event. If, however, it had been my decision to go out competitively I would have needed a different mental set. In the process of thinking through the race, I would have needed to add the ingredients of competition, pain, exact pacing, and the willingness to focus all my attention on the here-and-now system.

What equipment you use and the requirements for the transitions between events will depend specifically on the length and difficulty of the course. For sprint triathlons, most triathletes will swim in Lycra racing swimwear, slip into a pair of running or triathlon shorts and a pair of smooth-soled running shoes. This way, as soon as they finish the bike stage, they can begin the run without a change of clothing—saving a considerable amount of time. If, however, the bicycle portion is conducted over difficult terrain, it would be necessary to change into cleated cycling shoes. The new apparel that is designed specifically for triathlons should eliminate the need for changing corrals and the time wasted in this process. Recently, when I participated in the Monterey Triathlon, which included a 50-mile mountainous bicycle leg, I found myself in a poorly constructed changing corral that a gust of wind toppled over, leaving both men and women triathletes somewhat embarrassed. A friend who was photographing the triathlon found it more important to capture this part of the event on film than to rescue us from our predicament. So there are more reasons than just saving time to omit the hassle of having to change clothes during the race!

Race Tactics

The more you race, the more finely tuned to racing you become; you learn from experience and are able to use that information in subsequent competitive contests. Your initial commitment, then, is to learn how to race. It's no fun to make mistakes at first, and it costs you time in the race, so learn everything you can from your errors. An additional thing that you need to keep in mind is that not all triathlons follow the swim-bike-run sequence, and you therefore need to learn how to race with events scheduled in different combinations.

Two athletes can be in equally good physical condition and yet perform dramatically differently in the same race. A major difference between two individuals of otherwise equal ability can be a mental or psychological one. Mental toughness is a valuable trait and can pull you through some difficult situations. As I was climbing a difficult hill in Hawaii, to my pleasure and surprise, my training partner, Lori Brusati, brought her bicycle up next to mine and said, "Sally, you need to get down lower on your bike, spin faster, and, most of all, work hard." Since she was in the process of passing me, I considered her advice for a moment and thought that there might be something to it. I gritted my teeth and took her up on the last two words: work hard. For the balance of the event (about six hours), I repeated that mantra to myself. By focusing on those words and pushing myself through the pain, I fared well.

If you are a competitive triathlete, then you are going to have to find out for yourself the performance levels, the skills, and the racing tactics of other triathletes. Some are hares who sprint hard at the beginning and then slow down. Remember also that you

Kathleen McCartney demonstrates the kind of mental toughness that is required to "keep it all together" during competition.

are dealing with three different events and that your fellow competitors have different skill levels in all of them. This means that you can play cat-and-mouse catch-up games throughout the race, losing time in some events and picking it up in others. Remember that some athletes perform better when they race against themselves or against the clock, but that others need the stimulus of someone else near them to push or pull them through the race. You will need to learn what motivates *you* best, as well as what motivates your rivals.

In the pursuit of metallurgical victories, iron(wo)men sometimes carry with them an attitude that deserves mention. Among the different personality types, there seem to be those who believe that the spirit of camaraderie is superior to the attitude of cutthroat competition winner-takes-all. In the spirit of camaraderie, triathletes help fellow participants through positive reinforcement and words of encouragement. This group feels that if they offer positive vibrations to their fellow contestants, they will receive more in kind in return. On the other side is the spirit that sends the opposite kinds of vibrations through not only fellow competitors but through the sport itself. Recently, when I was wheezing up a long climb during the running leg of USTS–San Francisco triathlon in July 1982, I heard the sound of a man's voice, and as he passed I realized that he was chanting something to himself similar to my "work harder" mantra. His, though, was to repeat the word "kill" with each foot stride. I clearly got the message.

You must be able to supply a steady source of fuel to your body in order to maintain a high level of performance, particularly in middle-distance and ultradistance events. During the sprint triathlons, you will be able to depend solely on stored calories. What you eat or drink for the longer events is a highly individual matter, but what is important is that you supply nutrients and replacement fluids on a regular basis. Follow a prerace plan rather than depending on spur-of-the-moment decisions. During my 100-mile footraces, I have learned that it is important to have a variety of choices available to me as I proceed through the megahours of competition. My preferences have changed over the

A group of triathletes surging forward at the first leg of a triathlon. Most realize that the significance is not in what they attain, but rather in what they long to attain.

years, and I find that I now prefer fruit to candy, iced tea to cola drinks, and sandwiches to cookies.

Postrace Considerations

If you love to race frequently, then you must pay attention to the period of rest and recovery that needs to follow every race. A popular dictum is that you need an easy workout day for every mile that you race hard, before you give an all-out effort once more. If you run a hard marathon, for example, you shouldn't race hard again for a month. Some of postrace renewal, then, is physical. And there is often the sense, especially after a race that has required much mental and physical preparation, that you need some time off to get other things done in your life that have been waiting on the back burner. It's easy to get into the routine of pushing other things aside in favor of the demands of competition. You might need to get back to your family, your work, and your friends for a while. In postrace relaxation you should also incorporate new routines into your day—things like stretching, relaxation techniques, lighter eating, massage, and so on.

You may find it useful to review major races in writing: Put down how the race went for you, errors you made, things you forgot to prepare for, your highs and lows, changes you want to make. And don't forget to make note of the parts of the experience you really enjoyed. After the USTS–Long Beach triathlon I remembered my flat tire and the fact that I had no pump for my spare sew-up. First-time triathlete Mary Cavanaugh came up to me and offered me her pump or her bike in exchange for my lame 10-speed—that scene is still vivid in my memory. I took her pump gratefully, only to realize after she had departed that it didn't fit the type of valve I had on my tire. In desperation, I took off my wheel and ran through the crowd until I found assistance. I then returned to the scene of the disaster, put the wheel back on, and spun off. As I completed the balance of the race I chuckled aloud at how much fun I was having, especially now that I didn't have to worry about competing seriously!

FOR ULTRADISTANCE TRIATHLETES ONLY

Learning to mix the ingredients of equipment, nutrition, time budgeting, race tactics, and training progressions are all technical problems that you have mastered or will master with experience. If you have done an ultratriathlon, you know one thing that people who have only done shorter events want to know: how to change gears from short-distance races to longer ones. You already know that while the sprint triathlons require great intensity, the ultras require a great deal of relaxation, that you simply cannot stay intense—mentally or physically—for long periods of time. Most of you no longer think of the ultras in terms of distance; rather, you think in terms of amount of *time* you are going to be out on the course. Ultratriathletes constantly remind themselves of the finish time they have projected and how many hours they must remain in motion. With your mind's eye fixed on the finish, you can monitor the intensity of your efforts with greater ease.

Ultradistance triathlons would be frightening (and possibly physically destructive) if they were always approached with the intensity with which we race marathons. In *Ultramarathoning: The Next Challenge* (Anderson World, Mountain View, CA, 1980) Tom Osler suggests that it is possible to take a different approach to ultracompetitions. His advice is to go into the events in a joyous, cheerful manner, to look at them as celebrations of life and of the body's potential for energy, not as "gruelathons." And he has sage advice for what to do when things go wrong: it is a sign of common sense and mature self-control, he says, to stop the race when the conditions of pain and injury are too severe. Quitting in such instances is no loss of honor but rather a measure of the respect we show for our bodies.

For Osler, limping, staggering, and collapsing are not the gestures of the hero but are instead a sign that the body's energy reserves have been seriously misused. You should perform every triathlon with *class*, realizing your own strengths and limitations, understanding how they can best be utilized and not abused. The well-being of the body is too important, says Osler, to run one or two good races and spend the rest of life nursing a resulting injury. Osler's ultramarathoner's creed can be adapted equally well to the sport of triathlons.

Triathlete's Creed

1. I will respect my body as it is the source of my fitness. I will not subject it to foolish abuse but seek joy through its movement.

2. I will respond to my body's signal of being overtaxed (pain, discomfort, fatigue) by using the appropriate action of slowing down, resting, or quitting as the degree of these signals indicate.

3. I will enjoy triathlons and will make every effort to maintain this spirit in both competitive events and training.

4. I will serve as an example of the trained athlete. I realize that my appearance in competition and in training provides an example to others of what the triple-fit and healthy body can achieve. I will quit rather than allow the public to view a degrading display of overfatigue.

5. I will share with others the love of the sport of triathlons as the practitioner of whole-body aerobics. I will dispel the myth that triathlons are for crazies/overzealots/kamikazes/pain seekers.

This triathlon creed is designed to protect you, the competing athlete, from the death-at-all-costs syndrome, to protect the sport from the gladiators, the crowds, the splash of TV cameras in quest of the dying athlete, to protect the good name of the sport. The ultratriathlete has decided to show the world what the human frame is designed to do. The challenge of the great triathlete is to cover the miles and hours with dignity and pride—to perform with class.

appendix a: sources of information

SWIMMING

Organizations

COUNCIL FOR NATIONAL
COOPERATION IN
AQUATICS (CNCA)
220 Ashton Rd.
Ashton, MD 20702
(301) 924-3771

SWIMMING HALL OF
FAME, INC. (SHOF)
1 Hall of Fame Dr.
(305) 462-6536
(also address for the
AMERICAN COACHES
ASSOC.)

NATIONAL YOUNG
WOMEN'S CHRISTIAN
ASSOC. (YWCA)
600 Lexington Ave.
New York, NY 10022
(212) 753-4700

INTERNATIONAL AMATEUR
2000 Financial Center
Des Moines, IA 50309
(515) 244-1116

NATIONAL SWIMMING
POOL INSTITUTE
2000 K St. NW
Washington, DC 20006
(202) 331-8844

NATIONAL YOUNG MEN'S
CHRISTIAN ASSOC.
(YMCA)
291 Broadway
New York, NY 10007

Magazines

JOURNAL OF MASTERS
  SWIMMING
Dept. of PE
Western Illinois Univ.
Macomb, IL 61455

SWIM-MASTER
2308 NE 19th Ave.
Fort Lauderdale, FL 33305

SWIMMERS MAGAZINE
PO Box 15906
Nashville, TN 37215

MASTERS AQUATICS-
  CANADA
Whittall Publishing
PO Box 413
Schamberg, Ontario
Log Ito, Canada

SWIM SWIM
PO Box 5901
Santa Monica, CA 90405

SWIMMING TECHNIQUE
Swimming World Pub.
PO Box 45497
Los Angeles, CA 90045

BICYCLING

Organizations

BICYCLE INSTITUTE OF
  AMERICA
122 E. 42nd St.
New York, NY 10017

UNITED STATES CYCLING
  FEDERATION
Box 669
Wall Street Station
New York, NY 10005

INTERNATIONAL BICYCLING
  TOURING SOCIETY
846 Prospect St.
La Jolla, CA 92037

LEAGUE OF AMERICAN
  WHEELMEN
10 E. Read St.
Baltimore, MD 21202

AMERICAN BICYCLING
  ASSOCIATION
PO Box 718
Chandler, AZ 85224

Publications

AMERICAN CYCLIST
PO Box 11628
Milwaukee, WI 53211

VELO-NEWS
Box 1257
Brattleboro, VT 05301

BICYCLE PAPER
Box 842
Seattle, WA 98111

BICYCLE FORUM
PO Box 8311-K
Missoula, MT 59807

CYCLING USA
1750 E. Boulder
Colorado Springs, CO 80909
(The United States Cycling
Federation newspaper)

THE LAW BULLETIN
League of American
   Wheelmen
Box 988
Baltimore, MD 21203

RUNNING

Organizations

AAHPER: AMERICAN
   ALLIANCE FOR HEALTH,
   PHYSICAL EDUCATION,
   AND RECREATION
1201 16th St. NW
Washington, DC 20037
(Publishes pamphlets and
info on the benefits of
exercise and running)

AMERICAN RUNNING AND
   FITNESS ASSOCIATION
919 18th St. NW
Washington, DC 20006

AMERICAN HEART ASSOC.
7320 Greenville Ave.
Dallas TX 75231
(Free pamphlets on health
fitness running for both
runner and nonrunner)

ROAD RUNNERS CLUB OF
  AMERICA
1111 Army Navy Dr.
Arlington, VA 22202
(A national organization
that sponsors local
chapters to promote running
and racing in the local
community)

PRESIDENT'S COUNCIL ON
  PHYSICAL FITNESS &
  SPORTS
400 Sixth St., SW
Washington, DC 20201
(Sponsors the President's
Physical Fitness Awards
program, publishes booklets
for sale on various aspects
of fitness)

SENIOR SPORTS
  INTERNATIONAL
5225 Wilshire Blvd., Ste. 302
Los Angeles, CA 90036
(Sponsors the SENIOR
OLYMPICS for athletes
25 and over)

Magazines

THE AMERICAN JOURNAL
  OF SPORTS MEDICINE
428 E. Preston St.
Baltimore, MD 21202

ATHLETE'S WORLD
440-442 Whitmore Way
Basildon, Essex, England

CALIFORNIA TRACK AND
  RUNNING NEWS
Box 6103
Fresno, CA 93703

AMERICAN MEDICAL
  JOGGERS ASSOC.
  NEWSLETTER
Box 4704
North Hollywood, CA 91607

ATHLETIC JOURNAL
1719 Howard St.
Evanston, IL 60202

FITNESS
T. Fleming Associates
Box 4473
Pittsburgh, PA 15205

FOOTNOTES
11155 Saffold Way
Reston, VA 22090

MARATHON RUNNER
440-442 Whitmore Way
Basildon, Essex, England

NATIONAL MASTERS
  NEWSLETTER
102 W. Water St.
Lansford, PA 18232

THE RUNNER
1 Park Ave.
New York, NY 10016

RUNNING
Box 350
Salem, OR 97308

RUNNING TIMES
12808 Occoquan Rd.
Woodbridge, VA 22192

RUNNER'S WORLD
Box 366
Mountain View, CA 94042

THE HARRIER
Box 1550
Auburn, AL 36830

JOGGING
13 Golden Sq.
London W1R 4AG, England

MEDICINE and SCIENCE in
  SPORTS
1440 Monroe St.
Madison, WI 53706
(Journal of the American
College of Sports Medicine)

NEW ZEALAND RUNNER
Box 29-043
Aukland 3, New Zealand

THE PHYSICAL and
  SPORTSMEDICINE
4530 W. 77th St.
Minneapolis, MN 55435

RUNNING AND FITNESS
2420 K Street, NW
Washington DC 20037

SOVIET SPORTS REVIEW
Box 549
Laguna Beach, CA 92652

appendix b: statistics from october 1982 ironman triathlon world championship–hawaii

TOP 10 MEN FINISHERS

	Swim min/mile	Bike mph	Run min/mile	Total Elapsed Time hr/min/sec
Dave Scott	21.2*	21.7*	7:09*	9:08:23
Scott Tinley	25.4	21.1	7:14	9:28:28
Jeff Tinley	24.2	20.9	7:33	9:36:53
Scott Molina	22.0	20.6	8:04	9:50:23
Jody Durst	23.2	20.8	8:09	9:52:43
Kurt Madden	23.4	20.0	8:08	10:04:36
George Yates	28.2**	20.6	8:08	10:07:20
Dean Harper	22.3	19.4**	7:55	10:07:55
Reed Gregerson	23.1	19.8	8:11	10:08:24
Ferdy Massimino	22.3	20.4	8:42**	10:10:07

*Fastest pace.
**Slowest pace.

TOP 10 WOMEN FINISHERS

	Swim min/mile	Bike mph	Run min/mile	Total Elapsed Time hr/min/sec
Julie Leach	27.1	19.1*	9:06	10:54:08
Joann Dahlkoetter	30.9	18.5	8:28	10:58:21
Sally Edwards	31.5**	17.7	7:56*	11:03:00
Kathleen McCartney	30.8	19.1	9:21	11:10:53
Lyn Books	28.9	17.1**	8:12	11:18:14
Ardis Bow	24.9	18.5	9:52	11:21:58
Darlene Ann Drum	29.0	18.3	9:39	11:29:55
Kathie Rivers	28.4	18.2	9:39	11:29:55
Jennifer Hinshaw	22.3*	18.3	10:36**	11:38:08
Cheryl Lloyd	29.8	19.1	10:32	11:39:59

*Fastest pace.
**Slowest pace.

index